As one of the world's longest established and best-known travel brands, Thomas Cook are the experts in travel.

For more than 135 years our guidebooks have unlocked the secrets of destinations around the world, sharing with travellers a wealth of experience and a passion for travel.

Rely on Thomas Cook as your travelling companion on your next trip and benefit from our unique heritage.

Thomas Cook

Your travelling companion since 1873

Written by Sean Sheehan
Updated by Polia Mihaylova

Published by Thomas Cook Publishing
A division of Thomas Cook Tour Operations Limited
Company registration No: 3772199 England
The Thomas Cook Business Park, 9 Coningsby Road
Peterborough PE3 8SB, United Kingdom
Email: books@thomascook.com, Tel: +44 (0)1733 416477
www.thomascookpublishing.com

Produced by The Content Works Ltd
Aston Court, Kingsmead Business Park, Frederick Place
High Wycombe, Bucks HP11 1LA
www.thecontentworks.com

Series design based on an original concept by Studio 183 Limited

ISBN: 978-1-84848-306-4

First edition © 2006 Thomas Cook Publishing
This third edition © 2010 Thomas Cook Publishing
Text © Thomas Cook Publishing
Maps © Thomas Cook Publishing/PCGraphics (UK) Limited
Transport map © Communicarta Limited

Project Editor: Kelly Pipes
Production/DTP: Steven Collins

Printed and bound in Spain by GraphyCems

Cover photography (Traditional Bulgarian costume) © Nadia Mackenzie/Alamy

CONTENTS

INTRODUCING SOFIA

MAKING THE MOST OF SOFIA

THE CITY OF SOFIA

OUT OF TOWN TRIPS

PRACTICAL INFORMATION

INDEX

MAPS

SYMBOLS KEY

The following symbols are used throughout this book:

ⓐ address ⓣ telephone ⓦ website address ⓛ opening times
ⓝ public transport connections ⓘ important

The following symbols are used on the maps:

🄸 information office		▦ points of interest
✈ airport		○ city
✚ hospital		○ large town
🛡 police station		○ small town
🚌 bus station		▭ motorway
🚆 railway station		▭ main road
✝ cathedral		▭ minor road
❶ numbers denote featured		▭ railway
cafés & restaurants		

Hotels and restaurants are graded by approximate price as follows:
£ budget price ££ mid-range price £££ expensive

The following abbreviations are used for addresses:

Blvd	boulevard
Sq	square
St	street

▶ *View of Sofia from Mount Vitosha*

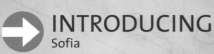

INTRODUCING
Sofia

Introduction

One of Europe's youngest capital cities – only established as such in 1879 – has all the attractiveness of precocious youth: unsophisticated, vigorously alive, relishing an undiluted urge for fun and late nights. Remarkably inexpensive bars, cafés, restaurants, pubs and piano bars are everywhere and closing times for all such places are commonly two in the morning, seven days a week. Less than a decade ago, no one could have imagined that staid and stodgy Sofia would morph into an epicurean outpost in the bleak Balkans. The metamorphosis is ongoing, and when you settle into a café-restaurant-bar – Sofia's secular trinity – you too become part of the process and start to soak up the unique character of this most surprising of European capitals.

Sofia is compact, and the hotels, restaurants and bars that will compete for your time are nearly all located within a tidily arranged city centre that is minutes from the airport. The city has a distinct European flavour with its broad boulevards and countless number of open-air watering holes, but there are intriguing reminders of its more Eastern heritage in the form of Byzantine- and Russian-inspired churches. The most immediate, and daily, reminder that that you are deep inside Eastern Europe comes when you grapple with street and place names that use the Cyrillic alphabet. It is part of the fun of being somewhere different, and you cannot get seriously lost because the city centre is too small. Trams and cheap taxis will take you anywhere that is not within walking distance.

What may at first seem a deficit of conventional attractions turns out to be a refreshing lack of manufactured tourism. There are museums and galleries to visit, but not so many as to exhaust yourself tramping from one must-see sight to another. Two or three days will easily cover the ground, and if your stay is any longer then it is time to take an excursion. There are two neighbouring towns with very contrasting characters, and the ski slopes at Mount Vitosha are a convenient six-minute bus ride away from one of the city's bus terminals.

🔺 *The city centre is filled with both historical buildings and green spaces*

When to go

As long as you have no objections to the snow and freezing temperatures of the winter months (when you can head to the ski slopes and warm up with hearty Bulgarian soups and stews), Sofia is a great place to visit at any time.

SEASONS & CLIMATE

Sofia's climate is continental, and while the summers are hot and sunny, the winter months can be very cold. January is the coldest, with the mercury dipping below zero at night, and the months either side are not noticeably different. This is certainly not a problem if skiing is on your agenda and you are above 800 m (2,625 ft) to enjoy blue skies and crisp snow. On sunny days, the daytime temperature can be 20°C (68°F) in the sun, though well below zero at night. Come March, temperatures start rising to around 5°C (41°F) and continue to rise steadily each month for the next three months.

April to June is a lovely time to be in Sofia, with alfresco eating and drinking being the order of the day; the weather is ideal for excursions into the countryside and airfares have not peaked. The public parks become attractions in their own right and are ideal for long picnics. In June the temperature is 19°C (66°F) and stays in the mid-20s°C (70s°F) throughout July and August, the hottest months of the year, until dropping back to June's average in September. Temperatures then plummet steadily each month, and by the end of November the first snow has fallen above 1,000 m (3,281 ft). December brings the freezing cold once more, and throughout the winter months Sofia is usually covered by a grey and heavy smog, making this period the least attractive time to make a visit (especially when fog causes flight delays at the airport).

ANNUAL EVENTS
January & February
Kukeri Men sporting hairy animal masks and cow bells perform dances aimed at driving away bad spirits and encouraging peace, health and fertility. Look out for them all over Sofia and Bulgaria between January and Easter.

March
International Women's Day (8 Mar) A day when the guys show the gals just how much they appreciate them.
Sofia International Film Festival The first half of March brings this festival, now well over ten years old and still going strong.
❶ (02) 916 6029 ⓦ www.cinema.bg/sff

April
Easter Easter according to the Eastern Orthodox calendar falls later than in the Catholic or Protestant churches. Midnight Mass is held, special food prepared and a festival of classical and choral music

MARCH & *MARTENITSAS*
At the start of March it is time to present friends and relatives with *martenitsas* – entwined red-and-white woollen threads – to bring them happiness and health. Sold everywhere, they are worn on clothing or tied around the wrist until, so the tradition goes, the first stork is seen. Sofia is not exactly overcrowded with storks, but by the end of the month people follow the custom of tying their *martenitsas* on to a fruit tree in a park or garden.

takes place in the city's churches.

Sofia Jazz Peak An international jazz festival showcasing real jazz legends as well as up-and-coming performers. As well as classic jazz, there's fusion, soul, world music and R&B. Takes place in April and November every year. Ⓦ www.sofiajazzpeak.org

May & June

Sofia Music Weeks A festival of symphonic and solo concerts, with local and international musicians performing mainly at Bulgaria Hall (see page 34).

🔺 *Fountains at the National Palace of Culture*

Salon of Arts The main venue for this culture fest is, appropriately, the National Palace of Culture (NDK, see page 95). Tickets can be bought in advance at the NDK ticket office.

December–April
The skiing season Come December, there is usually enough snow on Mount Vitosha (see page 116) to kick-start the skiing season. Most years, it effectively ends at the end of March, though it can linger into April.

PUBLIC HOLIDAYS
New Year's Day 1 Jan
Liberation Day 3 Mar
Easter Monday 25 Apr 2011, 16 Apr 2012, 6 May 2013
Labour Day 1 May
Bulgarian Army Day/St George's Day 6 May
Cyrillic Alphabet Day/Day of Bulgarian Education & Culture 24 May
Unification Day 6 Sept
Independence Day 22 Sept
Christmas Eve 24 Dec
Christmas 25 & 26 Dec

Banks, post offices, government offices and many shops and businesses are closed on public holidays, but restaurants and bars are not affected and public transport runs according to the usual schedules. If a public holiday falls on a weekend, the government may declare additional working days as public holidays.

Architectural affluence

The gift of beauty can often lead to an eventful life, and the greatest legacy of Sofia's undeniably tumultuous history is the huge number of fabulous buildings that are dotted all around the city. Its architectural spectrum encompasses an unusual mix that includes Byzantine-inspired churches and Soviet-influenced socialist art. Party House, the colonnaded former headquarters of the Central Committee of the Communist Party (see page 66), still asserts itself, in a butch architectural fashion at least, while only a short walk away stands a magnificent contrast in the neo-Byzantine form of the Alexander Nevsky Memorial Church (see page 80).

Equally impressive is the essentially art nouveau interior (though there are hints of Vienna Secession and, intriguingly, Moorish Revival) of the city's synagogue (see page 69), whose voluptuousness bears eloquent testimony to Bulgaria's tremendous act of protecting its Jewish population in World War II. The Soviet Army Monument (see page 106) is also tremendously affective. Although it is reviled by some Bulgarians because of the odious associations with the Soviet era that followed the end of World War II, it is a superb example of monumental sculpture and the best piece of public art in the city. Friezes around the base, depicting scenes of men and women fighting, are remarkably dynamic and convey a dramatic sense of movement. Confronting a brave new future, 34 m (111½ ft) above these scenes, a Red Army soldier stands in solidarity with a worker and a peasant woman with her child. The icing on the architectural cake takes high-spirited form in the neo-wacky Russian Church (see page 83), built in 1913 for an ultra devout diplomat from the soon-to-be-toppled Tsarist empire.

Trips out of the city will only add to your architectural pleasure. Koprivshtitsa, a small town 110 km (68 miles) to the east of Sofia, is noted for its traditional Bulgarian architecture, of which you'll find an enchanting example in Todor Kableshkov House (see page 138). The curvy lines of each side of its façade are a characteristic feature of the vernacular architecture. A cracking example of Bulgarian religious construction is found in the Rila Monastery (see page 130), whose fortress-like appearance and out-of-town location both attest to the beleaguered state of Christianity when Bulgaria was part of the Ottoman Empire (see page 14).

🔺 *Sofia Synagogue*

History

Bulgaria was known as Thrace to the ancient Greeks and to the Romans who conquered the land and made possible its incorporation into the Byzantine Empire that was ruled from Constantinople (Istanbul). Slavs migrated into the region and mixed with the nomadic Bulgars, laying the basis for a Bulgarian kingdom that succumbed to the power of the Ottoman Empire in the late 14th century. It was half a millennium later, with the help of Russian support for Slav independence, that a war of liberation against Turkish rule finally proved effective and the Treaty of San Stefano in 1878 recognised a liberated Bulgaria.

Bulgaria fell to the Nazis in World War II but, heroically and almost uniquely, Bulgarian public opinion resisted Nazi demands and the willingness of their Nazi puppet government for the country's Jews to be transported to the death camps. After the war, the Bulgarian Communist Party emerged to take political control and the country became part of the Soviet bloc under the dictatorial rule of Todor Zhivkov. The Cold War period gave Bulgarians guaranteed work and free medical care, but the country's image suffered in the West. The secret police were blamed for the murder of dissident writer Georgi Markov, stabbed on London's Waterloo Bridge in 1978 with a poison-tipped umbrella. Human rights campaigners drew attention to the persecution of racial minorities in Bulgaria itself. Sofia, none too surprisingly, was not a favourite holiday destination for Westerners.

The winds of change fanned by Gorbachev in Moscow swept into Bulgaria, and by the late 1980s economic and political life was beginning to change radically. As elsewhere in Eastern Europe, events moved swiftly and dramatically. On 10 November 1989, the day after the Berlin Wall came down, a power struggle and ideological split within the ruling party led to the removal of the old order – Zhivkov exited stage left – and the promise of free elections and a multiparty system. A new government emerged after elections in 1991, and the old system was dismantled. However, untamed capitalism led to a widening gap between rich and poor and to economic instability: by 1996, hyperinflation reached nearly 600 per cent. Street protests and strikes in 1997 led to a caretaker government and relative stability, although social divisions remained. In 2001, Simeon Saxe-Coburg Gotha, Tsar in exile after being expelled by the Communists, returned just two months before parliamentary elections. He formed a new party (National Movement Simeon II, now known as the National Movement for Stability and Progress) and won a landslide victory. In 2004, Bulgaria joined NATO, and in 2007 it became a full member of the EU.

In 2009 Boyko Borisov, former mayor of Sofia and chief secretary of the interior in Simeon II's government (and 7th dan black belt in karate), won the general elections with his young party GERB. He looks set to serve as prime minister of a centre-right government for the foreseeable future.

🔺 *Changing of the guard at the presidential offices*

Lifestyle

The lifestyle encountered in the city centre is recognisably that of continental Europe, characterised by a predominantly young population, with familiar brand names in the shop windows and advertisements for mobile phones. The pace of life may be slower than you are used to, and there is a pleasantly relaxed start to working days; weekends, by comparison, seem comatose. Young people learn English as their second language (their parents learned Russian), and their general level of education is high. While you cannot assume that English is generally understood, young people working in hotels and restaurants understand your needs and are usually more than willing to help.

While the lifestyle is Western European – and with a hedonistic vengeance when it comes to pavement cafés and bars – one aspect of Sofia that is decidedly Eastern is the alphabet. Sofia uses the Cyrillic alphabet, as used in Russia, Ukraine and Serbia with some minor variations. What will confuse you is that although some of the 30 letters look the same as Latin ones, they are pronounced very differently. A typical example is the word 'ресторант', which you will be tempted to pronounce as 'pectopaht' although it actually reads 'restaurant'. The briefest look at the Cyrillic alphabet (see page 56) will pay dividends when it comes to deciphering street and place names.

There is another lifestyle in Sofia, the one lived by an older generation that has had to cope with the momentous changes associated with the transition from a state-governed economy to a capitalist one, and the shift from a Balkan to a more Western European culture. It can be observed and appreciated in the Women's Market in the centre of the city (see page 74) – this is where ordinary people come to buy their clothes, food and other provisions – and here you will see the older lifestyle still ticking away. Shoppers in the market know how to judge the freshness of the fruits and vegetables on the stalls and they know the value of every cent. To enjoy and understand Sofia means acknowledging both these lifestyles.

● *Graffiti comes in Cyrillic, too*

Culture

The decades of subjugation under authoritarian, pro-Soviet governments fostered aspects of cultural development that were seen as intrinsically worthwhile but not threatening to the status quo. The legacy of this is that Sofia is home to a wealth of musical and theatrical establishments and, although the visitor that doesn't understand Bulgarian is handicapped when it comes to drama, there are wonderful opportunities to enjoy opera, ballet and classical music.

Spring, when musical festivities get underway, is the best time to enjoy these art forms although whatever the time of year, ticket prices are always wonderfully affordable. The Sofia Philharmonic Orchestra performs regularly, and the National Opera and Ballet has a repertoire of internationally recognised pieces. Musicals and operettas from *Die Fledermaus* to *Evita* are performed in the National Theatre, and although they are in Bulgarian they can still be hugely enjoyable.

Bulgaria's traditional culture is well represented at the National Ethnographic Museum (see page 72), housed in the former Royal Palace, which also plays host to international exhibitions. The most important collections, principally Thracian gold and silver treasures, have their home at the National History Museum (see page 109), situated at Boyana, to the south of the city, although the Thracian collection is often out of the country. In the same neighbourhood stands Boyana Church (see page 106), famous for its fragile frescoes from the medieval ages. Back in the city centre, the National Archaeological Museum (see page 72) has a number of interesting

● *Check out the sculptures at the Grita Gallery*

● *Detail from the façade of the National Theatre*

finds that date back to the time of ancient Greece and Rome.

The National Art Gallery is in Sofia (see page 72), but many visitors find more engaging art work in the National Gallery of Foreign Art (see page 84) and in smaller establishments like the Sofia City Art Gallery (see page 73), where changing exhibitions are likely to offer something interesting. New artistic endeavours, especially in painting and sculpture, are also to be found in a number of small, private galleries dotted around the city. In these galleries, original art work is for sale and often at very agreeable prices. This art scene is a shifting and developing one, but the relevant sections of the free city guides (see page 34) will highlight new galleries that have opened up and attracted attention.

● *The National Art Gallery and Ethnographic Museum*

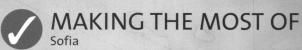

MAKING THE MOST OF
Sofia

Shopping

Shopping is an art form of its own in Sofia, and to find something interesting you often need to hunt down individual shops and stores. Fashionable Vitosha Boulevard, in the heart of the city, is a concentrated shopping area, particularly for clothing. It is pedestrianised, and so ideal for window shopping; a drawback for some, however, is that the outlets tend to focus on familiar Western brands. The same is true of TZUM (see page 74). Now a modern shopping mall, but once the state-owned department store, it's always justified its name, 'central universal shop' (the Bulgarian for which renders the abbreviated form 'Tzum').

Two other shopping centres are very popular. City Center Sofia (see page 110) and **Mall of Sofia** (❸ Alexander Stamboliyski Blvd 101 ❶ (02) 929 3377 ❿ www.mallofsofia.com ❶ 10.00–22.00) both have a great number of shops selling international brand-names, many cafés and restaurants, as well as modern multiplex cinemas. More rewarding in many ways is the narrow Tsar Shishman Street, which starts next to the Radisson Blu Grand Hotel (see page 42) and is home to a number of small, owner-run clothing boutiques with unique collections.

Pedestrianised Pirotska Street, where there are more boutiques, leads to the southern end of Zhenski Pazar, the Women's Market (see page 74). Crammed with stalls and shoppers, this is the place to buy a jar of fresh honey or stock up on your supply of vegetable seeds. The best market of all, in terms of finding something to bring home, is in front of the Alexander Nevsky Memorial Church (see page 80).

◐ Matryoshka *dolls for sale at the Alexander Nevsky Square Market*

For original Bulgarian art, the area worth exploring is around Parizh Street, close to the Alexander Nevsky Memorial Church and the National Opera and Ballet (see page 84). Here you will find a number of small galleries promoting the work of a new generation of young artists who work in a variety of styles from the expressive to the pictorial. An export licence may be required for some purchases, but the shops can arrange this.

Many shops in central Sofia accept credit cards, but some do not. Keep enough cash on you or ask before making a purchase to avoid embarrassment. Also bear in mind that Bulgarian clothing sizes are different from standard European ones, so do try on an item of clothing before buying it. Offering exchange and refund is not common practice in Bulgaria.

⬤ *Pedestrianised Vitosha Boulevard is the main shopping street in Sofia*

USEFUL SHOPPING PHRASES

What time do the shops open/close?
В колко часа отварят/затварят магазините?
V kolko chasa otvaryat/zatvaryat magazinite?

How much is this?
Колко струва това?
Kolko struva tova?

Can I try this on?
Може ли да пробвам това?
Mozhe li da probvam tova?

My size is...
Моят размер е...
Moyat razmer e...

I'll take this one, thank you
Ще взема това, благодаря
Shte vzema tova, blagodarya

**This is too large/too small/too expensive.
Do you have any others?**
Това е много голямо/малко/скъпо. Имате ли други?
Tova e mnogo golyamo/malko/skapo. Imate li drugi?

Eating & drinking

It is never a problem finding somewhere to eat and drink in Sofia. Prices are remarkably low, and often the more traditional Bulgarian dishes are preferable to Western European favourites. Standards of service vary, and you can be very pleased one day only to return another time and experience poor service, delays and confusion; this is all part of the city's learning curve rather than culpable lapses in standards. As a general rule, be as explicit as possible and try to check that your order has been understood.

Just about every menu begins with a list of various salads and among these there is nearly always a *shopska*. Almost a national dish, a *shopska* is made with chopped tomatoes, cucumber, peppers and onion, topped with white cheese. The *ovcharska* salad is similar but comes with grated egg and mushrooms. Equally popular is *snezhanka*, chopped cucumber with garlic mixed together in yogurt. For vegetarians, one of the salads followed by a hot starter makes

PRICE CATEGORIES
The following approximate price bands are based on the average cost of a three-course meal for one person, excluding drinks, and are indicated by these symbols:
£ up to 15lv   ££ 15–30lv   £££ over 30lv
In even the most expensive restaurants, you would seriously need to push the boat out in order to pay more than 50lv for a three-course meal.

● *Vitosha Boulevard from the Upstairs bar*

a suitable meal at lunchtime. Hot starters feature stuffed or roasted peppers and tend to avoid meat.

Soups feature on most menus and the ones most likely to appear include *bob chorba* (bean soup) and *shkembe chorba* (tripe soup). Vegetarians should look for *tarator* in the warm months – a refreshing, cold soup composed of yogurt and cucumber with garlic.

Main courses are usually based around meat, with chicken, pork and veal being the firm favourites, and grilled meats are very common. Expect to find *kyufteta* (meat balls), *parzhola* (chops) and *kebapcheta* (elongated meat balls). The choice of fish can be disappointing and usually comes down to *pastarva* (trout) and the seasonal offering from the Black Sea. Desserts are a real let-down, and finding yourself tempted by wicked chocolate concoctions is, sadly, all too rare an experience. However, ice cream is popular and of good quality.

Sofia has no shortage of places to drink, and even the humblest café or kiosk tends to stock a range of soft drinks, beers and spirits. Cappuccinos feature on many menus, but prepare to be disappointed when a powdery substance stirred limply into life with a modicum of froth arrives on your table. Regular coffee, which means espresso, may be too strong or just plain dire. Tea is widely available but unless you specifically ask for *cheren chay* (black tea), you will receive a herbal teabag without milk.

The most popular spirit is *rakiya*, a brandy made mainly from either plums or grapes. It is traditionally drunk with a salad as an aperitif and, with around 40 per cent alcohol (often more in the homemade versions), packs a punch. *Rakiya* and other spirits are listed in menus as 'small' (roughly equivalent to a British double) or 'large' (use your imagination), and there is often a variety of brands and prices to choose from. Burgas 63 is a good brand of grape *rakiya*,

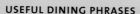

USEFUL DINING PHRASES

I would like a table for ... people
Бих искал маса за ... души
Bih iskal masa za ... dushi

Waiter/waitress!
Келнер!
Kelner!

Could I have it well-cooked/medium/rare please?
Може ли да го приготвите добре/средно/
леко опечено, моля?
Mozhe li da go prigotvite dobre/sredno/leko opecheno, molya?

I am a vegetarian. Does this contain meat?
Аз съм вегетарианец. Има ли месо в това?
Az sam vegetarianets. Ima li mesoh v tova?

Where is the toilet (restroom), please?
Къде е тоалетната, моля?
Kade e toaletnata, molya?

I would like a cup of/two cups of/another coffee/tea
Искам чаша/две чаши/още една чаша кафе/чай
Iskam chasha/dve chashi/oshte edna chasha kafe/chay

May I have the bill, please?
Сметката, моля?
Smetkata, molya?

while Troyanska is the best of the plum brandies.

Bulgarian wines are actually surprisingly good, particularly the red wines. Familiar grapes like Merlot and Cabernet Sauvignon have been grown in the country with notable success. Mavrud is a native grape variety which produces a hearty red wine with a 'beef-steak' quality. Wine lists in restaurants tend to be based around Bulgarian wines, and only the more expensive places will feature international selections. Half bottles are rarely listed on menus, but most places have no problem serving their wines by the glass. It's certainly worth trying a few local wines, if only out of interest – ask a local or the waiter for recommendations. You may be pleasantly surprised.

Bulgarian beers are palatable but not habit-forming, and imported Danish, German and Czech beers are available in almost all restaurants and bars.

Most restaurants are open seven days a week from around 10.00 or 11.00 to 23.00 or later. A service charge is not usually added to the bill and a tip of 10 per cent is normally expected – do check, however, as some restaurants now include a service charge. Meal prices are remarkably low by Western European standards and this goes some way in compensating for inconsistencies in standards and service. So if you do receive efficient, friendly service, feel free to leave a larger tip by way of encouragement.

A nationwide ban on smoking in public places took effect in June 2010, although what exactly constitutes a 'public place' is a subject of ongoing debate. Ask before lighting up.

◀ Bean casserole is a typical Bulgarian meal

Entertainment & nightlife

Sofia's entertainment scene is broadly night-based and you will be surprised at the sheer number of bars, nightclubs and pubs that light up after dark and remain busy until the early hours of the morning. There is the usual gamut of so-called Irish pubs and Buddha bars, but it is more interesting to seek out some of the small bars and clubs where young Bulgarians party away the night, and up-and-coming musicians try to make a breakthrough. The best way to find the latest hip venue or the 'next' Bulgarian rock band is to chat to young locals, but you can also look out for posters and adverts in listings magazines (see page 34). Piano bars are popular in a low-key kind of way, and provide a musical alternative to loud doses of pop rock.

There are no cover charges in most of the clubs, and there is usually a drinks list in English. The Bulgarian for 'cheers' is *nazdrave*, meaning 'good health' and, if you find yourself in a group toasting, etiquette demands that you clink your glass with each and every person in the group, looking them in the eye at the point of clinking. Failing to do so is taken as a lack of politeness.

Music usually takes the form of *chalga* – shaking up the body and waggling limbs to a hybrid ethno-pop sound. In visitor-oriented restaurants staff are decked out in Arabian Nights costumes, but the shows are not as tacky as you might fear. Where some caution should be exercised is with the more lurid-looking nightclubs that obviously aim to draw in an adult male audience; it is not unknown for a hapless punter to be landed with a heavy bill and given no option but to pay up. The casinos that announce their presence in neon are best only patronised by the experienced.

One of the more positive legacies of the Soviet era is Sofia's deep interest in ballet and classical music, and there are many opportunities to enjoy it – particularly since tickets are amazingly affordable compared to Western countries. Check the listings magazines (see page 34) or ask at the tourist office for details of current shows and performances. Tickets are best booked in person at the relevant theatre's box office, which should usually be open 10.00–18.30 (sometimes closed between 13.30 and 15.30).

The main venue for classical performances is the National Palace of Culture, or NDK (see page 95) with its 3,800-seat main hall and many smaller concert spaces. Throughout the year, it hosts a variety

● *Sofia City Garden, home to the National Theatre and Bulgaria Hall*

WHAT'S ON?

The *Insider's Guide* is a free listings magazine that appears every three months, and copies should be available in your hotel. There is also a free monthly *City Info Guide* that covers the same ground. Both these guides carry their own useful maps of the city area. Every Friday, the English-language *Sofia Echo* appears and carries current listings of what's on at the cinemas and details of theatrical and musical events.

See ⓦ www.programata.bg for current information on Sofia's cultural, entertainment and nightlife scene.

of cultural events. The **Bulgaria Hall** (ⓐ 1 Aksakov St ① (02) 987 5237 ⓦ www.sofiaphilharmonie.bg) is home to the Sofia Philharmonic Orchestra. The National Opera and Ballet performs in their impressive namesake building on Vrabcha Street (see page 84).

Rock and pop concerts by big-name stars such as Madonna and Metallica take place at the **Vasil Levski National Stadium** (ⓐ Evlogi Georgiev Blvd 38 ① (02) 930 0666), in Borisova Gradina (see page 104). With a capacity of 44,000, it is the largest stadium in Bulgaria.

Hollywood films, shown in the original version with subtitles in Bulgarian, are shown regularly in cinemas, and ticket prices average about 8lv. The main cinema complexes are the nine-screen **Cineplex** (ⓐ City Center Sofia shopping mall (see page 110) ① (02) 964 3007) and **Cinema City** (ⓐ Mall of Sofia (see page 22) ① (02) 981 1911 ⓦ www.cinemacity.bg ① 10.00–00.00), with 12 screens and a 3D cinema.

● *Alexander Stamboliyski, 1920s prime minister, by the National Opera and Ballet*

Sport & relaxation

SPECTATOR SPORTS

Sofia's biggest spectator sport is football, and its two biggest teams are **Levski** (🅦 www.levski.bg) and the Bulgarian Army club team, **CSKA** (🅦 www.cska.net). Levski play at the **Georgi Asparuhov Stadium** (🅐 Todorini Kukli Street 47 🅣 (02) 847 8134) in the northeast of the city. CSKA play at the **Balgarska Armiya Stadium** (🅐 Entrance off Dragan Tsankov Blvd 3 🅣 (02) 963 4279), on the southern side of Borisova Gradina (see page 104). Tickets for local matches can be

⬤ *Snowboarders waiting for the bus to Mount Vitosha*

bought at the door on the day of the match. International fixtures take place at the Vasil Levski National Stadium (see page 34), also in Borisova Gradina.

PARTICIPATION SPORTS

When Bulgaria's cold winter arrives, skiing is the thing to do. Mount Vitosha (see page 116) is only a bus ride from the city centre. Between December and April, thick snow cover provides good ski runs – with a total length of 29 km (18 miles) – that serve both beginners and more experienced skiers. There are several ski schools at Aleko, situated just above the tree line, offering lessons for absolute beginners from the age of six upwards. From Aleko, a chair lift and several drag lifts take you up to the higher runs. You can hire all the necessary gear by the day.

Outside winter the area is popular with hikers, with trails criss-crossing the mountain. There is a chairlift from the village suburb of Dragalevtsi as well as a cable car from Simeonovo. On the more wooded western side of the mountain, Zlatni Mostove is an outdoor area that is a good picnic spot in the summer. If you go there on a weekday, you will have plenty of space to yourself and you can explore the huge boulders that line the course of the river.

If all that sounds a little too energetic, get a group together for ten pin bowling at Sofia's **Galaxy Bowling Club** (ⓐ Bulgaria Blvd 1 ❶ (02) 916 6590 ⏱ 10.00–02.00).

RELAXATION

Sofia has a number of parks, but the one that offers the most in the way of relaxation is Borisova Gradina (see page 104). This is the largest park in the city, and an hour or more could easily be spent wandering its paths; it is also suitable for jogging.

Accommodation

There is a good range of accommodation in Sofia, from hostels to 5-star opulence, and you should be able to stay close to the city centre. Some good, mid-range hotels, like the Lozenetz (see page 39), are just a little outside the city centre but still within walking distance – a tram ride or an inexpensive taxi-ride away. Expect some quirks as even the best hotels can fail when it comes to brown bread for breakfast, and a toaster may be missing from an otherwise good 3-star place. This sounds like carping, but prices are comparable to Western European ones where standards are higher.

It is best to make internet bookings in advance, either directly with the hotel or through an accommodation website like Ⓦ www.sofiahotels.net or Ⓦ www.hotelsinsofia.com. A buffet breakfast is included in the room rates. Tea- and coffee-making facilities are not usually available in hotel rooms, but mini-bars are in many mid-range hotels, and a safety deposit box is either in the room or available at reception. English-speaking staff in all the hotels listed here are usually very helpful when it comes to calling a taxi for you or dealing with day-to-day enquiries.

HOTELS

California £ Lovely place, a little outside the centre in Lozenetz. A variety of rooms plus sauna, room service, internet access and a restaurant in traditional Bulgarian style. ❷ Bigla St 30 (Outside the centre) ❶ (02) 962 9300 Ⓦ www.hotelcaliforniasofia.com

Madrid £ Small hotel in a quiet street ten minutes' walking distance from the centre. The rooms are simply furnished but tidy and comfy. ❷ Dragovitsa St 12 (Outside the centre) ❶ (02) 944 8952 Ⓦ www.madridbg.com

PRICE CATEGORIES

The following price guides indicate the approximate cost of a room for two people for one night, including tax and breakfast unless otherwise stated.

£ up to 150lv ££ 150–300lv £££ over 300lv

Niky £ Quiet location off Vitosha Boulevard, with good-value singles and doubles plus 17 suites with kitchenettes. Free internet and pleasant restaurant. ⓐ Neofit Rilski St 16 (Around Vitosha Boulevard) ⓣ (02) 952 3058 ⓦ www.hotel-niky.com

Pop Bogomil £ Situated in an area of cobbled streets and close to the city centre. Rooms are smallish and decorated a little kookily, but are basically comfortable. Rooms with a bath need requesting in advance. ⓐ Pop Bogomil St 5 (Around Alexander Nevsky Memorial Church) ⓣ (02) 983 1165

Tzar Asen £ Seven rooms in a quiet suburban setting. ⓐ Tsar Assen St 68 (Around Vitosha Boulevard) ⓣ (02) 954 7801 ⓦ www.hotel-tzar-asen.hit.bg

Lozenetz £–££ Just south of the city centre, this is a modern and classy hotel with a good restaurant, friendly staff and Wi-Fi. ⓐ Sveti Naum Blvd 23 (Outside the centre) ⓣ (02) 965 4444 ⓦ www.lozenetzhotel.com

Art 'Otel ££ One block away from Vitosha Boulevard, this hotel has over 20 rooms, some of which offer cityscape views. ⓐ Gladstone St 44 (Around Vitosha Boulevard) ⓣ (02) 980 6000 ⓦ www.artotel.biz

Arte ££ In the heart of Sofia, this offers stylish furnished rooms with flat-screen TVs and Wi-Fi. ⓐ Knyaz Alexander Dondukov Blvd 5 (Around Sveta Nedelya Square) ⓣ (02) 402 7100

Central ££ On the west side of the city, with 25 rooms that all have Wi-Fi. A bar, restaurant, sauna and laundry service feature among its attractions. ⓐ Hristo Botev Blvd 52 (Around Sveta Nedelya Square) ⓣ (02) 981 2364 ⓦ www.central-hotel.com

⬤ *The elegant Sheraton Sofia*

Diter ££ A smart hotel in a quiet location with excellent facilities, including safe and mini-bar. Well managed; restaurant downstairs.
ⓐ Han Asparuh St (Around Vitosha Boulevard) ⓣ (02) 989 8998
ⓦ www.diterhotel.com

Legends ££ Medium-sized, intimate hotel 3 km (nearly 2 miles) south of the centre, with convenient transport links to the city centre and very close to Hladilnika bus station for catching a bus to Vitosha. Reasonable prices for the stylish facilities and comfort.

ⓐ Cherni Vrah Blvd 56 (Outside the centre) ⓣ (02) 961 7930
ⓦ www.hotel-legends.bg

Light ££ Located in a quiet, cobbled street, but central; a touch of class in the contemporary décor but most rooms have only a shower.
ⓐ Veslets St 37 (Around Sveta Nedelya Square) ⓣ (02) 917 9090
ⓦ www.hotels.light.bg

Sveta Sofia ££ Attractive and central location. ⓐ Pirotska St 18 (Around Sveta Nedelya Square) ⓣ (02) 981 2634 ⓦ www.svetasofia-alexanders.com

Arena di Serdica ££–£££ An excellent base for sightseeing and with a fantastic view from its rooftop restaurant. Spacious rooms, huge beds and bathrooms, plus plasma TVs and Wi-Fi. ⓐ Budapeshta St 2–4 (Around Alexander Nevsky Memorial Church) ⓣ (02) 810 7777
ⓦ www.arenadiserdica.com

Hilton Hotel £££ Reliably first class, with free use of pool and gym, and a good restaurant; situated behind the NDK. ⓐ Bulgaria Blvd 1 (Outside the centre) ⓣ (02) 933 5000 ⓦ www.sofia.hilton.com

Radisson Blu Grand Hotel £££ A great location opposite Alexander Nevsky Memorial Church, and one of the best places to stay.
ⓐ Narodno Sabranie Sq 4 (Around Alexander Nevsky Memorial Church) ⓣ (02) 933 4334 ⓦ www.radissonblu.com

Sheraton Sofia Hotel Balkan £££ A landmark hotel when it opened in the mid-1950s, and now a classic with its high ceilings, marble columns and stately staircases. ⓐ Sveta Nedelya Sq 5 (Around Sveta Nedelya Square) ⓣ (02) 981 6541 ⓦ www.luxurycollection.com

APARTMENTS

Apartment House Dunav £–££ Fourteen fully furnished comfortable apartments decorated in neutral colours with equipped kitchenettes. Friendly and attentive staff. The rates fall substantially the longer you stay. ⓐ Dunav St 38 (Around Alexander Nevsky Memorial Church) ⓣ (02) 983 3002 ⓦ www.dunavapartmenthouse.com

HOSTELS

Art Hostel £ More than just a bed for the night – a cultural centre and art gallery with a relaxing garden where you can chat to young English-speaking locals. ⓐ Angel Kanchev St 21A (Around Vitosha Boulevard) ⓣ (02) 987 0545 ⓦ www.art-hostel.com

HostelMostel £ Bunk-bed accommodation in dorms in a hostel which has more living space than most. Floor space is also sometimes available if you have your own sleeping bag. ⓐ Makedonia Blvd 2A (Around Sveta Nedelya Square) ⓣ 0889 223296 ⓦ www.hostelmostel.com

Kervan Hostel £ Comfortable and cosy hostel to the north of Alexander Nevsky Memorial Church and close to the Opera House. ⓐ Rositsa St 3 (Around Alexander Nevsky Memorial Church) ⓣ (02) 983 9428 ⓦ www.kervanhostel.com

Sofia Guest House £ A quiet, well-run place with simple but clean rooms, a short way out from the city centre. There's a spacious social area, breakfast room and TV. Good value. ⓐ Patriarh Evtimiy Blvd 27 (Outside the centre) ⓣ (02) 403 0100 ⓦ www.sofiaguest.com

THE BEST OF SOFIA

Whether you're on a flying visit to Sofia or taking a more leisurely break in Bulgaria, the city offers sights and experiences that should not be missed.

TOP 10 ATTRACTIONS

- **Alexander Nevsky Memorial Church** Neo-Byzantine extravaganza and, outside, a great street market (see page 80)

- **Borisova Gradina** Sofia's largest park with ponds and paths and non-urban vibes (see page 104)

- **Boogying at the Bibliotekata** Underneath the National Library, there's live music... and a sushi bar. That's a library (see page 89)

- **Frescoes in Boyana Church** Unique frescoes from the 13th century, comparable to the achievements of the early Italian Renaissance (see page 106)

- **Rila Monastery** Bulgaria's best monastery – a day trip from Sofia (see page 130)

- **Sofia's pub-restaurants** A plethora of alfresco bars serving food through a long summer's night (see pages 26–31)

- **Women's Market** Balkan flavours in Sofia's most traditional market, where you can find everything from carrots to broomsticks (see page 74)

- **Skiing and hiking around Mount Vitosha** The snow-capped mountain that can be seen from the city centre is ideal for for outdoor sports (see page 116)

- **Banya Bashi Mosque** The city's only functioning mosque takes its name from the magnificent mineral baths nearby (see page 66)

- **Sofia Synagogue** A mix of Byzantine and Moorish styles, designed by an Austrian, and with – wait for it – the biggest chandelier in the Balkans (see page 69)

◑ *Bulgarians and Russians meeting in victory, 1944*

Suggested itineraries

HALF-DAY: SOFIA IN A HURRY

There is enough time to walk the city centre and see the main sights. Start outside the Radisson Blu Grand Hotel (see page 42) and cross the cobbled square, past the white parliament building, to the Alexander Nevsky Memorial Church (see page 80) and its golden domes. The crypt houses a priceless collection of icons, while out in the public square vendors retail World War II memorabilia and assorted artefacts. A short walk westwards, along Tsar Osvoboditel Boulevard, passes the stunning little Russian Church (see page 83) and its five golden onion domes, then the National Art Gallery (see page 72) and the Ethnographic Museum (see page 72). They are on Alexander Batenberg Square, where troops once goose-stepped and tanks rolled by in convoys during the Stalinist era. Appropriately enough, you soon find yourself gazing up at the Party House (see page 66), former headquarters of the Communist Party. You are now on the west side of the city and close to Tsentralni Hali – an indoor market with a choice of places to eat (see page 75).

● *Parliament building*

1 DAY: TIME TO SEE A LITTLE MORE

The half-day itinerary opposite could be followed, after leaving Tsentralni Hali, by a visit to the city's attractive synagogue (see page 69) and then a stroll down the pedestrianised Pirotska Street, which leads to the Women's Market (see page 74). You may purchase very little, but the authentic flavour of the Balkans is gradually disappearing in the capital and it can still be experienced for real here. There is also time for a quick walk past the church of Sveta Nedelya (see page 70) and a look at the shops in Vitosha Boulevard. You could end the day in style by enjoying a Bulgarian-style meal at the fabulous Pod Lipite (see page 113) restaurant and taking a short stroll down to the live-music nightclub, Swingin' Hall (see page 114).

2–3 DAYS: TIME TO SEE A LOT MORE

The first day, or day-and-a-half, could be occupied with the suggestions above, while the extra time would allow for a day trip out of the city centre to the National History Museum (see page 109) or Boyana Church (see page 106). It takes less than an hour to reach Mount Vitosha (see page 116), and you would also have time for a day's skiing or a hike on the mountain. The nights give you time to drop in on some more of the city's bars and restaurants.

LONGER: ENJOYING SOFIA TO THE FULL

You can do all of the above and still have time to experience the full Top 10 Attractions (see page 44). Spend a day exploring bucolic Koprivshtitsa (see page 136) and the town's traditional Bulgarian architecture (see page 12) and/or, in a more hedonistic spirit, take an excursion to the bars of Blagoevgrad. A trip to fortress-like Rila Monastery (see page 130) could also be on your itinerary.

Something for nothing

Sofia's great churches are free to enter and so you can explore Alexander Nevsky Memorial Church (see page 80), though there is a small charge to view the crypt. The National Gallery of Foreign Art (see page 84) is free on Mondays. The city's parks are free, and Borisova Gradina (see page 104) always makes a relaxing destination on a fine day. At the junction of Vitosha Boulevard and Patriarh Evtimii Boulevard, NDK Garden is not a very green space, and Sofia City Garden (see page 69) is a more peaceful place to take a rest; if you fancy your chess skills, feel free to challenge one of the players who regularly use part of the park.

Sofia has a compact city centre and the following walk costs nothing but takes in many sights. Start outside Sveta Nedelya Church (see page 70) and walk north up Maria Luiza Boulevard to Pirotska Street. Walk down pedestrianised Pirotska Street and at the end turn to the right to enter the Women's Market (see page 74). After exploring the market, retrace your steps to Maria Luiza Boulevard and cross to the other side, and head back the way you came. After passing the giant TZUM shopping mall (see page 74), turn left into Nezavisimost Square, and you immediately see the magisterial Party House (see page 66) looming ahead. Cross to the other side so that you keep Party House on your left as you walk into Alexander Batenberg Square and the City Garden (see page 69) on your right. There are several open-air summer café-bars around the **National Theatre** (ⓐ Dyakon Ignatiy St 5 ❶ (02) 811 9227 ⓦ www.nationaltheatre.bg) in the park. After a rest in the park, walk back to Alexander Batenberg Square and, facing the park, the former royal palace that now houses the National Art Gallery (see page 72) and the National Ethnographic Museum (see page 72).

A short walk eastwards along Tsar Osvoboditel Boulevard brings you to the delightful St Nicholas Russian Church (see page 83). Continue along the boulevard until you come to the Radisson Blu Grand Hotel (see page 42) and Narodno Sabranie Square. From here you can see the Alexander Nevsky Memorial Church (see page 80) on your left. After leaving the church, continue eastwards along Tsar Osvoboditel Boulevard and cross to the other side. Here stands the Monument to the Soviet Army, the best example of Communist sculpture in Sofia.

◗ *Frieze around the base of the Monument to the Soviet Army*

When it rains

All the churches and museums can be visited on a wet day and, as many of them are close to one another, you need only an umbrella to keep safely dry. From the Alexander Nevsky Memorial Church (see page 80) it takes less than five minutes to reach the Russian Church (see page 83). Almost next door, the National Art Gallery (see page 72) and the Ethnographic Museum (see page 72) are conveniently together in a former royal palace. Opposite the Russian Church there is a comfortable café to enjoy a break, and from here it is a five-minute walk to the Archaeological Museum (see page 72).

The Sofia Synagogue (see page 69), the Banya Bashi Mosque (see page 66) and the church of Sveta Nedelya (see page 70) are also near one another. Time inside these buildings could be combined with some window shopping in the TZUM shopping mall (see page 74) and, across the street, Tsentralni Hali (see page 75), where food and drink is also available.

A wet day provides an opportunity to visit some of the smaller museums and galleries dotted around the city. The foyer of the **Russian Cultural Centre** (🏛 Shipka St 34 ☎ (02) 943 3693 🕐 10.00–18.00 Mon–Fri) is home to a virtually life-size model of the Vostok-3 capsule that sent Yuri Gagarin into space.

By way of entertainment, a visit to the cinema will escape the rain and the cinema complex, in the City Center Sofia shopping mall (see page 110), is a short walk from the rear of the Hilton Hotel (see page 42).

A trip to the National History Museum (see page 109) would take up at least half of one wet day although, to avoid the rain, a taxi ride there and back would be best. Whatever the weather, Sofia's countless bars are always open, and if you stayed in the vicinity of Tsar Ivan

Shishman Street, it would be easy to pop from one to another without getting too wet.

⬤ *The imposing Banya Bashi Mosque*

On arrival

TIME DIFFERENCE
Sofia is on Eastern European Time, two hours ahead of Greenwich Mean Time (GMT). Between the end of March and the end of October, clocks are put forward by one hour for Daylight Saving Time.

ARRIVING
By air
Sofia International Airport (☎ (02) 937 2211 🌐 www.sofia-airport.bg) is 10 km (7 miles) east of the city centre. It is relatively small for a European capital with just two terminals but has the basic facilities: ATMs, bank offices, car hire counters, cafés and desks for booking a taxi. Ignore the taxi touts and, after using the ATM machine, book a taxi for the short journey into town. The fare will be around 15lv.

Between 05.00 and 23.00, buses 84 (from Terminal 1) and 284 (from Terminal 2) run to Orlov Most Square, east of the city centre. You need to purchase a ticket (around 1lv) from the kiosk near the bus stop before boarding the bus or from the bus driver. If you have a lot of luggage, you have to buy separate tickets for every piece bigger than 60 x 60 x 40 cm (otherwise you could be fined).

By rail
Sofia's **Central Station** (☎ (02) 931 1111 🌐 www.bdz.bg 🕐 04.00–01.00) is an ugly concrete shelter north of the city centre on Maria Luiza Boulevard. It is a 20-minute walk from here to Sveta Nedelya Square. Alternatively, take tram lines 1 or 7 (purchase your ticket from the kiosk before boarding). ATMs and left-luggage facilities are available at the station. Beware of meter scams from taxi drivers hanging around the station; it may be worth walking the short distance to the bus station and catching one there.

IF YOU GET LOST, TRY ...

Excuse me, do you speak English?
Извинете, говорите ли английски?
Izvinete, govorite li angliyski?

**Excuse me, is this the right way to... the cathedral/
the tourist office/the old town?**
Извинете, това ли е пътят за... катедралата/
туристическото бюро/стария град?
*Izvinete, tova li e patyat za ... katedralata/
turisticheskoto byuro/stariya grad?*

Can you point to it on my map?
Може ли да ми покажете на моята карта?
Mozhe li da mi pokazhete na moyata karta?

By road

The **Central Bus Station** (☎ 0900 21000 🌐 www.centralbusstation-sofia.com 🕐 06.00–00.30), 200 m (219 yds) east of the railway station on Maria Luiza Boulevard, is a well-organised place with good facilities, including ATMs, left-luggage facility, food court, information desk and a taxi-booking kiosk. It is a 20-minute walk away from Sveta Nedelya Square, or a short tram ride on lines 1 or 7.

FINDING YOUR FEET

Sofia is a safe city to travel around and the pace of life is not frantic. The difficulty is grappling with the Cyrillic alphabet. Finding a menu

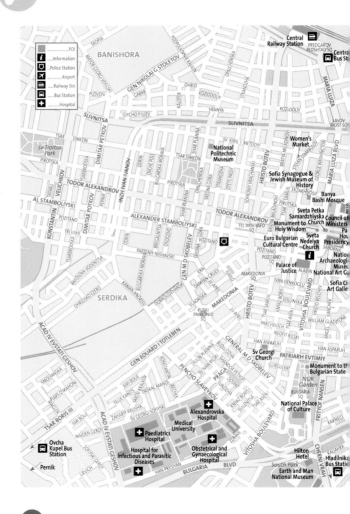

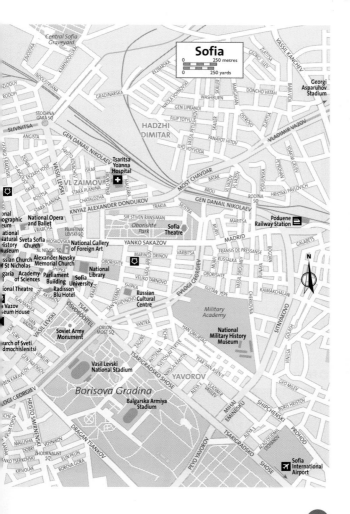

in English is not difficult, but a sign or street name is more elusive, and it is good to have at least a nodding acquaintance with the alphabet.

THE CYRILLIC ALPHABET

Аа	a as in cat
Бб	b as in bus
Вв	v as in very
Гг	g as in go
Дд	d as in door
Ее	e as in bet
Жж	zh like the s in leisure
Зз	z as in zoo
Ии	i as in bit
Йй	y as in yes
Кк	k as in kit
Лл	l as in like
Мм	m as in met
Нн	n as in net
Оо	o as in got
Пп	p as in pot
Рр	r as in rasp
Сс	s as in see
Тт	t as in tip
Уу	u as in rule
Фф	f as in fruit
Хх	h as in hand
Цц	ts as in cuts
Чч	ch as in chip
Шш	sh as in ship
Щщ	sht like the last syllable in joshed
Ъъ	u as in but
Юю	yu as in you
Яя	ya as in yarn
ь	softens 'o' as in yoga

● **РЕСТОРАНТ ГРОЗД** = *RESTAURANT GROZD*

🔺 Catch a tram

ORIENTATION

The use of the Cyrillic alphabet for street names makes orientation
a little more difficult than it would otherwise be, and it pays
to study a map before setting out for any destination. If you get
confused about which street you are on, ask someone for directions
– a young person is more likely to speak English – or enquire in
a shop. The main tram routes are often helpful in orientating
yourself, and major landmarks include the National Palace of
Culture (NDK, see page 95). Traffic drives on the right and usually
stops for pedestrians at zebra crossings, but be careful and do not
take this for granted.

GETTING AROUND

The city centre is small and compact enough to get around mostly on
foot, and this is by far the most enjoyable option. Trams, trolleybuses

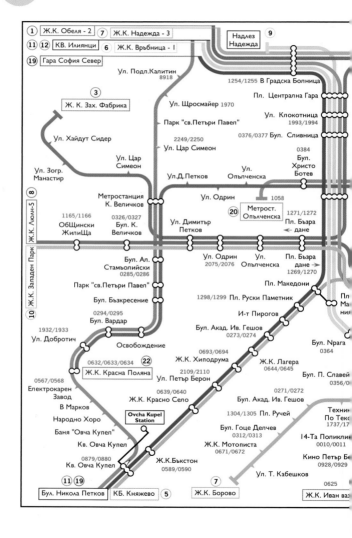

① Ж.К. Обеля - 2 ⑦ Ж.К. Надежда - 3

⑪ ⑫ КВ. ИЛИЯНЦИ ⑥ Ж.К. Връбница - I

⑲ Гара София Север

Надлез Надежда ⑨

Ул. Подп.Калитин 8918

1254/1255 В Градска Болница

Пл. Централна Гара

③

Ж. К. Зах. Фабрика

Ул. Щросмайер 1970

Ул. Клокотница 1993/1994

Парк "св.Петри Павел"

Ул. Хайдут Сидер

2249/2250

0376/0377 Бул. Сливница

Ул. Цар Симеон

0384 Бул. Христо Ботев

Ул. Зогр. Манастир

Ул. Цар Симеон

Ул.Д.Петков

Ул. Опълченска

Ул. Одрин 1058

Метростанция К. Величков

Ул. Одрин

1271/1272

⑳ Метрост. Опълченска

1165/1166 0326/0327

Пл. Бъзра дане ←

ОбЩински ЖилиЩа

Бул. К. Величков

Ул. Димитър Петков

Бул. Ал. Стамьолийски 0285/0286

Ул. Одрин 2075/2076

Ул. Опълченска

Пл. Бъзра дане → 1269/1270

Парк "св.Петри Павел"

Пл. Македони

Бул. Бъзкресение

1298/1299 Пл. Руски Паметник

Пл Ма ния

0294/0295 Бул. Вардар

И-т Пирогов

1932/1933 Ул. Добротич

Бул. Акад. Ив. Гешов 0273/0274

Освобождение

Бул. Nрага 0364

0632/0633/0634 ㉒

0693/0694 Ж.К. Хиподрума

Ж.К. Лагера 0644/0645

Ж.К. Красна Поляна

2109/2110 Ул. Петър Берон

Бул. П. Славей 0356/0

0567/0568 Електрокарен Завод

0639/0640 Ж.К. Красно Село

0271/0272 Бул. Акад. Ив. Гешов

Техни По Тек 1737/17

В Марков

1304/1305 Пл. Ручей

Народно Хоро

Ovcha Kupel Station

Бул. Гоце Делчев 0312/0313

14-Та Полкли 0010/0011

Баня "Овча Купел"

Ж.К. Мотописта 0671/0672

Кино Петьр Б 0928/0929

Кв. Овча Купел

0879/0880 Кв. Овча Купел

Ж.К.Бъкстон 0589/0590

Ул. Т. Кабешков

0625

⑪ ⑲

Бул. Никола Петков КБ. Княжево ⑤

⑦ Ж.К. Борово

Ж.К. Иван ваз

⑧ Ж.К. Люми-5

⑩ Ж.К. Западен Парк

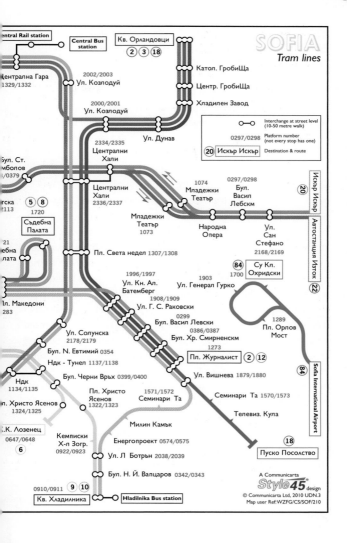

SOFIA
Tram lines

Central Rail station

Central Bus station

Кв. Орландовци
② ③ ⑱

Катол. ГробиЩа

Центр. ГробиЩа

Хладилен Завод

Централна Гара
1329/1332

Ул. Козлодуй
2002/2003

Ул. Козлодуй
2000/2001

Ул. Дунав

Централни Хали
2334/2335

Бул. Ст. ѕмболов
0/0379

Централни Хали
2336/2337

Младежки Театър
1074

0297/0298
Бул. Васил Лебскм

⑳

Искър Искър

Автостанция Изток

②②

тѕка
⑤ ⑧
113
1720

Съдебна Палата

21
ѕебна лата

Младежки Театър
1073

Народна Опера

Ул. Сан Стефано
2168/2169

Interchange at street level
(10-50 metre walk)

0297/0298
Platform number
(not every stop has one)

⑳ Искър Искр   Destination & route

Пл. Света недел 1307/1308

Ул. Кн. Ал. Батемберг
1996/1997

Ул. Генерал Гурко
1903

Ул. Г. С. Раковски
1908/1909

Бул. Васил Левски
0299

Бул. Хр. Смирненскм
0386/0387

⑧④ Су Кл. Охридски
1700

Пл. Орлов Мост
1289

⑧④

Sofia International Airport

Пл. Македони
283

Ул. Солунска
2178/2179

Бул. N. Евтимий 0354

Ндк - Тунел 1137/1138

Пл. Журналист ② ⑫
1273

Ул. Вишнева 1879/1880

Ндк
1134/1135

Бул. Черни Връх 0399/0400

ѕп. Христо Ясенов
1324/1325

Пл. Христо Ясенов
1322/1323

Семинари Та
1571/1572

Семинари Та 1570/1573

Телевиз. Кула

.К. Лозенец
0647/0648

⑥

Кемписки Х-л Зогр.
0922/0923

Милин Камък

Энергопроект 0574/0575

Ул. Л Ботрън 2038/2039

⑱ Пуско Посолство

Бул. Н. Й. Вапцаров 0342/0343

A Communicarta
Style45 design
© Communicarta Ltd, 2010 UDN.3
Map user Ref:WZFG/CS/SOF/210

0910/0911 ⑨ ⑩

Кв. Хладилника

Hladilnika Bus station

and regular buses criss-cross the city and are a reliable means of getting around if you know where to get off. There is one metro line running from the western suburb of Lyulin to the eastern suburb of Mladost via the city centre. It is useful for getting from Sveta Nedelya Square to Sofia University or the National Stadium. There are also private minibuses that drop passengers off at any point along their set route, but unless you meet a local who can explain the routes this can prove confusing. Taxis are plentiful and inexpensive and can be booked in advance.

The city's trams and buses are often old, grubby and slow, but services are reliable and run from around 05.00 to 23.30. Tickets need to be purchased from kiosks (such as newspaper kiosks) near bus stops before boarding and they are validated on the tram or bus by inserting them into one of the mechanical puncher machines on the wall. Single-journey tickets cost 1lv, but a strip of five tickets costs 4.50lv and ten tickets 8lv, saving you time and money. With a strip of five or ten tickets, the rule is that they must be used in sequence and those numbered 1–9 (or 1–4) are not valid unless you still have the last, un-punched one, in your possession. Travel passes are also available: for one day they're 4lv, for five days 15lv and for one month 50lv. The challenge, though, is to find the bus or tram stop because they are often unmarked and you may have to look for likely groups of passengers waiting for a bus. Tram stops are sometimes in the middle of the road and passengers wait on the pavement until the tram approaches.

Registered taxis, painted bright yellow, are easy to find and use digital meters. There are disreputable taxi companies that will overcharge, but as long as you use the companies listed here there should be no problem. Oval sticker on the windscreen, driver's ID card, car number and table of fares should be clearly displayed, but

◔ *A tram passes through the cobbled streets of Sofia*

● Ask your hotel staff if you need help with transportation

most drivers do not speak English. Taxis can be booked in advance and reception staff at your hotel are usually happy to call one for you and, if necessary, explain to the driver where you want to go. Three reliable taxi companies are:

OK Supertrans ❶ (02) 973 2121
Taxi S Express ❶ (02) 912 80
Radio CB Taxi ❶ (02) 912 63

CAR HIRE

Car hire is hardly worth the trouble of organising when public transport serves the excursion destinations, although a car would be helpful for Rila Monastery (see page 130). **Avis** (Ⓦ www.avis.bg) and **Hertz** (Ⓦ www.hertz.bg) have offices at the airport and in the city.

▶ The rooftops of Sofia

THE CITY OF
Sofia

Around Sveta Nedelya Square

Sveta Nedelya Square can be regarded as the centre of the city and a major orientation point when you first start exploring it. It is a compact area and everywhere can be reached on foot. Vitosha Boulevard, the main shopping street, runs due south from the square, while immediately to the north stands the landmark Monument to Holy Wisdom. The main way east leads almost immediately to Nezavisimost Square, also known as the Largo, and this leads to the attractions on the east side of the city. The main street heading north from Sveta Nedelya Square is Maria Luiza Boulevard and it heads towards the bus and railway station. Although Maria Luiza Boulevard accesses some sights, principally the synagogue (see page 69), it is not long before this street becomes decidedly grotty and the way to the bus and railway stations becomes one of the least attractive thoroughfares in the city.

SIGHTS & ATTRACTIONS

Alexander Batenberg Square
The square near the Party House used to be called the Ninth of September Square, commemorating the date of the Communist takeover in 1944, and it was the focal point for government-related parades until 1989. There used to be a giant mausoleum facing the square, holding the embalmed body of Georgi Dimitrov, the country's first Communist leader. The Bulgarian politburo would stand on the mausoleum to take the salute from goose-stepping troops and the convoys of tanks that rolled by over the cobbles. Dynamite removed the mausoleum in 2000, but ideas for replacing the site with something attractive were not followed through and dull shrubbery covers the ground.

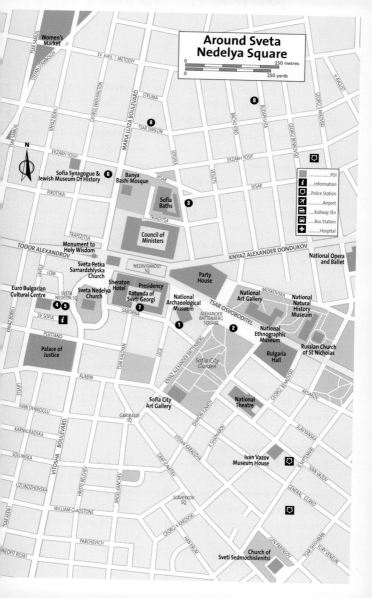

Around Sveta Nedelya Square

| 0 | | | 250 metres |
| 0 | | | 250 yards |

Women's Market

SV. KIRIL I METODIY

STEFAN STAMBOLOV

TSAR SAMUIL

KNYAZ BORIS

GEORGE WASHINGTON

MARIA LUIZA BOULEVARD

STRUMA

❾

BUDAPESTA

GEORGI S. RAKOVSKI

RAKOVSKI

TSAR SIMEON ❽

SERDICA

BACHO KIRO

EKZARH YOSIF

TSAR SAMUIL

Sofia Synagogue & ❻
Jewish Museum Of History

Banya
Bashi Mosque

IKSAR

VESLETS

EKZARH YOSIF

IKSAR

PIROTSKA

Sofia
Baths ❸

TRAPEZITSA

TODOR ALEKSANDROV

Monument to
Holy Wisdom

TRIADITSA

Council of
Ministers

KNYAZ ALEKSANDER DONDUKOV

National Opera
and Ballet

Sveta Petka
Samardzhiyska
Church

NEZAVISIMOST
SQ

Party
House

National
Art Gallery

MOSKOVSKA

Euro Bulgarian
Cultural Centre

SVETA
NEDELYA SQ

❹❺

Sveta Nedelya
Church

Sheraton
Hotel

Presidency
Rotunda of
Sveti Georgi ❼

SABORNA

National
Archaeological
Museum ❶

ALEKSANDER
BATTENBERG
SQUARE

❷

TSAR OSVOBODITEL

National
Natural
History
Museum

National
Ethnographic
Museum

Russian Church
of St Nicholas

SV. SOFIA

ℹ

POZITANO

KNYAZ ALEKSANDER BATTENBERG

Sofia City
Garden

Bulgaria
Hall

AKSAKOV

Palace of
Justice

LAVELE

LOM

KNYAZ BORIS

TSAR KALOYAN

ALABIN

DIMAN CANEV

Sofia City
Art Gallery

GARIBALDI
SQ

National
Theatre

GEORGI S. RAKOVSKI

SLAVYANSKA

IVAN DENKOGLU

LAVELE

VITOSHA BOULEVARD

HRISTO BELCHEV

ANGEL KANCHEV

STEFAN KARADZHA

GRAF IGNATIEV

K. SHAPKAREV

Ivan Vazov
Museum House

❖

6 SEPTEMVRI

IVAN VAZOV

KARNIGRADSKA

SOLUNSKA

UZUNDZHOVSKA

WILLIAM GLADSTONE

STAVEYKOV
SQ

GENERAL GURKO

TSAR ASEN

NEOFIT RILSKI

PARCHEVICH

GEORGI S. RAKOVSKI

HAN KRUM

Church of
Sveti Sedmochislenitsi

GEN. PARENSOV

TSAR SHISHMAN

TSAR IVAN SHISHMAN

❖

Legend

	POI
ℹ	Information
⊖	Police Station
✈	Airport
🚉	Railway Stn
🚌	Bus Station
✚	Hospital

N

Banya Bashi Mosque

The only city mosque still in use, this takes its name from the nearby
mineral baths (*banya bashi* means 'many baths') and dates back to
the 16th century. The architect was Hadji Mimar Sinan, the leading
Muslim designer of the age and creator of some magnificent edifices
outside Bulgaria, but on this project he contented himself with a
single large dome and one minaret. Notwithstanding the modesty
of the design, the mosque is a singularly attractive addition to the
city centre. The mineral baths behind the mosque, closed to the
public, were built in the early 20th century and rate as one of the
architectural highlights of the city. ⓐ Maria Luiza Blvd ⓛ 08.00–17.00
ⓘ Visitors welcome except at prayer times, expect least access on
Fridays; women should be modestly dressed

Party House

A short walk from the Sheraton Hotel (see page 42) onto Nezavisimost
Square immediately brings into view Party House, the large, neoclassical
building that was once the headquarters of Bulgaria's Communist
Party. The building looks powerful, and was even more so when it
sported a giant red star on its summit. The star was removed in
August 1990 when protestors tried to set it on fire. Party House
now contains offices of the National Assembly and is closed to
the public. ⓐ Nezavisimost Sq

Rotunda of Sveti Georgi

Easy to miss, tucked away behind the Sheraton Hotel, Sofia's oldest
church stands in a small courtyard. The red-brick exterior looks
uninspiring and only its fourth-century Roman origins would seem
to impart significance to the building, but step inside to view some
stunning 14th-century frescoes and a depiction of wise men that

The Rotunda of Sveti Georgi

dates from the 10th and 12th centuries. The church became a mosque during the Ottoman period, and the frescoes, painted over, remained hidden until the 20th century. ⓐ Behind Sheraton Hotel (see page 42); access via Saborna St ⓣ (02) 980 9216 ⓦ www.svgeorgi-rotonda.com

Sofia City Garden

Immediately south of Alexander Batenberg Square, the pretty stretch of green that constitutes Sofia City Garden comes into its own with the advent of spring. Local office workers take advantage of the sunshine during their breaks, and chess players settle into studied silence after setting their game clocks. There is more than one place serving drinks and the elegant neoclassical façade of the National Theatre (see page 48) bestows an air of cultural refinement on the park scene. ⓐ South of Alexander Batenberg Sq ⓛ 24 hrs

Sofia Synagogue

Designed and built in the first decade of the 20th century, this elegant and imaginative synagogue is a reminder that in the past one in five of the city's citizens were Jews. Austrian architect and designer Friedrich Gruenanger boldly mixed Moorish and Byzantine features around a large octagonal dome and multiple turrets. The art nouveau-style interior contains a giant brass chandelier weighing over 2,200 kg (4,410 lb). Built to house 1,300, attendances now number less than 75; the city's Jews mostly emigrated in the late 1940s. There is a museum upstairs (see page 70). ⓐ Ekzarh Yosif St 16 ⓣ (02) 983 5085 ⓦ www.sofiasynagogue.com ⓛ 08.30–16.30 Mon–Fri; ring bell for caretaker if door closed; small charge for depositing bags

ⓞ *Ceremony preparation in the Sveta Nedelya Church (see page 70)*

Sveta Nedelya Church

The present church in Sveta Nedelya Square occupies a spot where a succession of churches has stood since medieval times. The location is associated with a Serbian king, Stefan Urish, whose bones are believed to have the power to perform miracles and are preserved in a wooden box to the right of the iconostasis. The church you see today was built in the mid-19th century, and in 1925 it survived a bombing attempt to eliminate the Bulgarian royal family, who were in the church attending a funeral. Although 193 mourners were killed and the building badly damaged, the royals escaped unhurt. ⓐ Sveta Nedelya Sq 20 ⓣ (02) 987 5748 ⓛ 07.00–19.00; daily liturgies at 08.00 & 16.00

Sveta Petka Samardzhiyska Church

Situated in the subway next to the Sheraton Hotel (it wasn't found until the end of World War II), this is one of the few medieval churches in Sofia to have survived to the present day. *Samardzhiyska* means 'of the saddlemakers', and this is apt as this is where such craftsmen used to hold their rituals. ⓐ Nezavisimost Sq ⓛ 09.00–17.00

CULTURE

Jewish Museum of History

On the second floor of the beautiful Sofia Synagogue (see page 69) is a museum focusing on the Jewish communities of Bulgaria and the rescue of Bulgarian Jews during World War II. ⓐ Ekzarh Yosif St 16 ⓣ (02) 983 1440 ⓦ www.sofiasynagogue.com ⓛ 08.30–12.30, 13.00–16.30 Mon–Fri. Admission charge

◍ *National Theatre, Sofia City Garden*

National Archaeological Museum

A modest but engaging collection of Thracian, Greek and Roman remains and some medieval artefacts from around the country. The more spectacular exhibits include a Thracian gold burial mask from the fourth century BC that was excavated in 2004. There is also a gravestone from the sixth century BC, found at the site of an ancient Greek colony on the Black Sea coast. Directly across the cobbled street from the museum's entrance are the offices of the Bulgarian president. The entrance is fronted by guards in fancy 19th-century dress, and on the hour they do a quick pirouette routine. ⓐ Saborna St 2 ⓣ (02) 988 2406 ⓦ www.naim.bg ⓛ 10.00–18.00. Admission charge

National Art Gallery

The other half of the former royal palace housing the Ethnographic Museum constitutes the National Art Gallery. The galleries downstairs are devoted to temporary exhibitions of contemporary Bulgarian art, the quality of which varies, while the main galleries use their space to good effect in highlighting the best Bulgarian artists of the past. Look for the work of Vladimir Dimitrov-Maystora (1882–1960), Bulgaria's greatest artist of the 20th century. His paintings of peasant girls in bucolic settings are strangely alluring because of a near-mystical quality endowed by the colours. ⓐ Alexander Batenberg Sq 1 ⓣ (02) 980 3325 ⓦ www.nationalartgallerybg.org ⓛ 10.00–18.00 Tues–Sun. Admission charge

National Ethnographic Museum

Reflecting Bulgarian culture through the centuries, the collections of Balkan arts and crafts that make up this museum are housed in one half of the former royal palace and this explains why features of the building's interior design, the plasterwork especially, are themselves an attraction of any visit. The particular theme behind a special exhibition that is showcased while you are in the city may help you to decide whether to make a visit or not. Unlike some of the city museums, the exhibits are all explained in English. ⓐ Alexander Batenberg Sq 1 ⓣ (02) 987 4191 ⓛ 10.00–18.00 Mar–Oct; 10.00–17.00 Nov–Feb. Admission charge

Sofia City Art Gallery

Constantly changing profiles of either contemporary Bulgarian artists or international shows; the information sheets are not in English but with free admission you have nothing to lose by popping in to view the works. ⓐ Gurko St 1 ⓣ (02) 987 2181 ⓦ www.sghg.cult.bg ⓛ 10.00–19.00 Tues–Sat, 11.00–18.00 Sun

RETAIL THERAPY

Bulgarski Dyukyan A cornucopia of kitchenware that sells Balkan crockery, embroidered tablecloths and peasant-style copper pots. ⓐ Pirotska St 11 ⓛ 09.30–19.30 Mon–Fri, 10.00–17.00 Sat

Ethnographic Museum Shop Bulgarian kilims are one of the better buys, but there's also jewellery, folk artefacts and Bulgarian music. You do not need to visit the museum to check out the shop (which, incidentally, also opens on Mondays, when the museum itself is closed). ⓐ Alexander Batenberg Sq 1 ⓣ (02) 987 4191 ⓛ 10.00–18.00

Stenata Their stock of hiking, camping and climbing gear is the best in the city. Walk west along Alexander Stamboliyski Boulevard from Sveta Nedelya Square, and Bratya Miladinovi Street is the fourth

PIROTSKA STREET & WOMEN'S MARKET

Pirotska Street, one block south of the street where Sofia Synagogue stands (see page 69), is a pleasant pedestrianised street with small shops occupying old buildings that date back a century or more. At the end of this street, a right turn at the junction where trams cross leads directly to the Women's Market, or Zhenski Pazar, a dense but not claustrophobic open-air bazaar. Farmers sell their fresh produce alongside stalls retailing inexpensive clothing, broomsticks for the home and assorted items. The market has atmosphere and a character that is quite at odds with the air of sophistication being promoted in the rest of the city. ⓐ Stefan Stambolov St ⓛ Women's Market: 08.00–19.00

street on your left. ⓐ Bratya Miladinovi St 5 ⓣ (02) 980 5491 ⓦ www.stenata.com ⓛ 10.00–20.00 Mon–Fri, 10.00–18.00 Sat

TZUM Once the consumer showpiece of Communist-era Sofia, now fulfilling a similar function for the post-Communist bourgeoisie of the city: three levels of boutiques, accessories, cosmetics and foreign newspapers. There's also a café and restaurant. ⓐ Maria Luiza Blvd 2 ⓣ (02) 926 0614 ⓦ www.tzum.bg ⓛ 10.00–21.00 Mon–Sat, 11.00–20.00 Sun

TAKING A BREAK

Art Club Museum £ ❶ Tucked away at the back of the Archaeological Museum and attracting a sophisticated-looking set of customers, this is an ideal spot for coffee and cakes or something more substantial. For added interest, head downstairs to where the seating rubs shoulders with ancient gravestones. Wi-Fi connection. ⓐ Saborna St 2 ⓣ (02) 980 6664 ⓛ 24 hrs

Bulgaria £ ② A very swish café, carpeted, with large glass windows for street-watching. Have a posh frappé or Viennese coffee with helpings of tiramisu, strudel or blackberry pie. The truffle and white chocolate dessert also tempts the palate. ⓐ Tsar Osvoboditel Blvd 4 ⓣ (02) 988 5307 ⓛ 08.30–23.00

Classic £ ③ This pizza restaurant is located just five minutes' walk from Sveta Nedelya Square in a tiny street near the Party House. The simple (but pleasant) interior, a reliable range of pizzas and salads, friendly service and Wi-Fi make it great for a break. ⓐ Serdika St 14 ⓣ 0878 656401 ⓛ 11.00–00.00

Flocafe £ ④ International-style lounge bar and restaurant offering a good choice of coffee, fresh sandwiches, fancy cakes and cookies. Wi-Fi connection. ⓐ Sveta Nedelya Sq 3 ⓣ (02) 950 6645 ⓛ 08.00–01.00

Happy Bar & Grill £ ⑤ The interior décor: neon-lit guitars alongside rock and movie posters on the walls, and laminated menus; a bright and cheerful joint for drinks or a quick meal from the menu of grills, chicken and countless salads. There's another branch at Rakovski St 145. Wi-Fi connection. ⓐ Sveta Nedelya Sq 4 ⓣ (02) 980 7353 ⓛ 24 hrs

Tsentralni Hali £ ⑥ On the top floor of this restored market hall there is a food court with various options or, in the basement, a branch of the always-reliable Trops Kushta. ⓐ Maria Luiza Blvd 25 ⓣ (02) 917 6111 ⓛ 07.30–22.00

AFTER DARK

RESTAURANTS

Kumbare ££ ❼ Everything you could expect from a Greek restaurant – plenty of grilled lamb and fish dishes accompanied by abundant salads, all prepared under the watchful eye of a head chef from Thassos. The chandeliers and Ionian columns only add to the Mediterranean vibe. ⓐ Saborna St 14 ⓣ (02) 981 1794 ⓦ www.kumbare.com ⓛ 11.00–00.00

⬥ *Upstairs at Sin City*

L'Etranger ££ ❽ An intimate restaurant that offers delicious dishes, perfectly prepared and arranged by the French chef. The desserts are real gems. ⓐ Tsar Simeon St 78 ❶ (02) 983 1417 ⏱ 12.00–15.00, 18.00–22.00 Mon–Fri, 18.00–22.00 Sat

Otvad Aleyata Zad Shkafa £££ ❾ One of the most elegant and atmospheric restaurants in Sofia. The menu is a tad extravagant for some, but all the dishes are delicious and look like real works of art. Excellent service, too. ⓐ Budapeshta St 31 ❶ (02) 983 5545 ⏱ 12.00–00.00

NIGHTLIFE

Gramophone Retro Club Join a stylish clientele in this trendy bar and nightclub. The drinks menu offers a dazzling array of cocktails for all tastes and price ranges. ⓐ Budapeshta St 6 ❶ (02) 981 1410 ⏱ 24 hrs

Sin City The city's biggest entertainment complex, consisting of pop-folk, house and retro music halls as well as a piano bar and café. Modern flashy interiors and high-quality sound systems. ⓐ Hristo Botev Blvd 61 ❶ (02) 810 8888 ⏱ 21.00–06.00. Admission charge

Toba & Co Tucked away to the rear of the National Art Gallery is this odd little joint that turns into a swinging venue when the right kind of DJ is on the decks. ⓐ Moskovska St 6 ❶ (02) 989 4696 ⏱ 10.00–03.00

Around Alexander Nevsky Memorial Church

Immediately north of Tsar Osvoboditel Boulevard is Alexander Nevsky Memorial Church (see page 80). Tsar Osvoboditel Boulevard itself leads to Narodno Sabranie Square, another landmark location for orientation purposes, identified by the curving façade of the Radisson Blu Grand Hotel (see page 42). Tsar Shishman Street, the first turning on the left with your back to the entrance of the Radisson, is an important street for accessing bars, restaurants and shops in this area.

SIGHTS & ATTRACTIONS

Graf Ignatiev Street

Graf Ignatiev Street is an extremely busy – by Sofia's standards – tram-laden thoroughfare that cuts across the city centre from near Sveta Nedelya Square towards the southeastern outskirts of the capital. It is named in honour of the Russian count, who was the grandfather of the novelist Michael Ignatiev. Graf Ignatiev was instrumental in getting Tsar Alexander III to take on the Ottoman Empire and thus liberate Bulgaria. Graf Ignatiev Street crosses Slaveikov Square, where there is an enjoyable open-air book market, before arriving at one of the city's main fruit and vegetable markets. At the point where Graf Ignatiev Street meets Tsar Shishman Street, which runs northeast up to the Radisson Blu Grand Hotel, stands the church of Sveti Sedmochislenitsi.

Narodno Sabranie Square

Tsar Osvoboditel Boulevard connects Sveta Nedelya Square in the west of the city with Narodno Sabranie Square (National Assembly Square) in the east. This large cobbled area is defined on its north

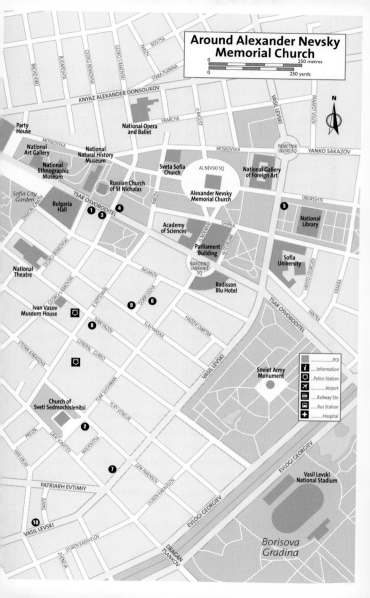

Around Alexander Nevsky Memorial Church

0 ———————— 250 metres
0 ———————— 250 yards

N

GEORGI BENKOVSKI
GEORGI S RAKOVSKI
PARIN
ROSITSA
STARA PLANINA
BACHO KIRO
BUDAPESHTA
GEORGI BENKOVSKI

KNYAZ ALEXANDER DONSOUKOV

VRABCHA
II AUGUST
VASIL LEVSKI
PANAYOT VOLOV

Party House

MOSKOVSKA

National Art Gallery

National Ethnographic Museum

National Opera and Ballet

National Natural History Museum

MOSKOVSKA

PAMETNIK LEVSKI SQ

YANKO SAKAZOV

Sveta Sofia Church

AL NEVSKI SQ

National Gallery of Foreign Art

Russian Church of St Nicholas

Sofia City Garden

DYAKON IGNATII

TSAR OSVOBODITEL

Bulgaria Hall

Alexander Nevsky Memorial Church

❹

❶ ❸

PARIZH

OBORISHTE

❺

National Library

Academy of Sciences

SHIPKA

National Theatre

GEORGI BENKOVSKI

Parliament Building

NARODNO SABRANIE SQ

Sofia University

HRISTO GEORGI

KRAKRA

VANTKA

TSAR OSVOBODITEL

AKSAKOV

S SEPTEMVRI

❾ ❻

DOBRI VODA

Radisson Blu Hotel

HADZHI DIMITAR

VASIL LEVSKI

Ivan Vazov Museum House

🄿

IVAN VAZOV

❽

SLAVYANSKA

GENERAL GURKO

🄿

STEFAN KARADZHA

YURIY VENELIN

TSAR SHISHMAN

Soviet Army Monument

Church of Sveti Sedmochislenitsi

❷

GRAF IGNATIEV

MALYOVITSA

GEN GURKO

GEN ABENSOV

❼

PRESP.

HAN KRUM

PATRIARH EVTIMIY

LYUBEN KARAVELOV

EVLOGI GEORGIEV

Vasil Levski National Stadium

DANTE

ZHENSKA

❿

VASIL LEVSKI

LYUBEN KARAVELOV

EVLOGI GEORGIEV

DRAGAN TSANKOV

Borisova Gradina

.... POI
ℹ ... Information
🄿 ... Police Station
✈ ... Airport
🚉 ... Railway Stn
🚌 ... Bus Station
✚ ... Hospital

ALEXANDER NEVSKY MEMORIAL CHURCH

Russian architects, principally Alexander Pomerantsev from St Petersburg, designed this church in the 1880s (building was completed in 1924), with the conscious aim of emulating the architectural glory of Byzantium. They undoubtedly succeeded because the result is a masterpiece that magnificently balances multiple gold-leafed domes to create an aesthetically pleasing structure. It was built to commemorate Russia's costly contribution to Bulgaria's liberation – countless thousands of Russians died fighting in the 1877–8 War of Liberation – and the money was raised by public subscriptions. The name of the church, however, refers to the subject of Eisenstein's famous film, a 13th-century prince who helped preserve Novgorod's independence.

The atmospheric interior is generously decorated with dynamic frescoes illuminated by numerous candles flickering in the darkness and enriched by onyx and alabaster columns adorning the thrones in the iconostasis. ⓐ Alexander Nevsky Sq ⓣ (02) 988 1704 ⓒ Visits: 07.00–19.00; daily prayers: 08.00 & 17.00; vigil: 18.30 Sat; mass: 09.30 Sun

side by the country's parliament building and, facing it on the south side in front of the Radisson Blu Grand Hotel, a 14 m (46 ft) monument depicting Tsar Alexander II of Russia on horseback. The tsar is honoured because it was his declaration of war on the Ottoman Empire that led to Bulgarian independence. Those who actually did the fighting are represented in the reliefs around the pedestal.

▶ *Alexander Nevsky Memorial Church with a sprinkling of snow*

⬥ *Golden domes of the Russian Church of St Nicholas*

Russian Church of St Nicholas

The Russian theme continues with this highly photogenic and
spirited creation gracing Tsar Osvoboditel Boulevard. The green
steeple and the perfectly proportioned golden onion domes create
an effervescence that is cheerfully at odds with the dour concrete
that makes up so many of the buildings on this thoroughfare.
The church was built in the early 20th century to serve the city's
Russian elite and would not look out of place in the Kremlin. The
interior is dark and mysterious, filled with the scent of burning
candles and incense. ⓐ Tsar Osvoboditel Blvd 3 ⓣ (02) 986 2715
ⓒ 08.30–18.30

Sveta Sofia Church

Sitting in the shadow of Alexander Nevsky Memorial Church (see
page 80), this brown brick church is the second-oldest building
in Sofia, and it's had a fascinating life. Constructed on the site of a
Roman theatre, its first incarnation was as a fifth-century basilica.
During Ottoman rule, the church was converted into a mosque and
the original 12th-century frescoes were destroyed. After the 1878
liberation, it was restored and reinstated as a church. Outside,
to the left of the main entrance, stands the Monument to the
Unknown Soldier, lit by a perpetual flame in honour of those who
died for Bulgaria. ⓐ Parizh St 2 ⓣ (02) 987 0971 ⓒ 09.00–18.00

CULTURE

Crypt of Alexander Nevsky Memorial Church

The unrivalled collection of icons in the church's crypt is from all parts
of the country, a result of scouring obscure churches and isolated
monasteries, and covering almost a millennium in time. The majority

of icons date from the last two centuries; the rarest are unique examples of medieval iconography; and a common pictorial theme is of the warrior saints George and Demetrius slaying dragons – a coded representation of the struggle against Ottoman oppression. ⓐ Entrance to the left of the church doors in Alexander Nevsky Sq ⓣ (02) 981 5775 ⓛ 10.00–18.00 Tues–Sun. Admission charge

National Gallery of Foreign Art

Eclectic is the best way to describe what is on show, and the chances are that you will find something surprising and rewarding. The Asian art from Burma and Japan makes up the most gratifying exhibits for many visitors. Minor European art includes a Picasso lithograph, drawings by Delacroix and Renoir, and a bewitching piece by Franz von Stick. The basement contains a fourth-century Roman tomb. ⓐ Alexander Nevsky Sq 1 ⓣ (02) 988 4922 ⓦ www.foreignartmuseum.bg ⓛ 11.00–18.30 Wed–Mon. Admission charge (free Mon)

National Natural History Museum

An absolute treat of a museum, especially for children. It houses a great collection of fossils and mammals, hundreds of species of birds and thousands of insects. Although most of them are stuffed and pickled, there are also many live reptiles. A small gift shop sells fantastic souvenirs including minerals and fossils. ⓐ Tsar Osvoboditel Blvd 1 ⓣ (02) 987 5115 ⓦ www.nmnhs.com ⓛ 10.00–18.00. Admission charge

National Opera and Ballet

Built in 1909 and seating 1,200, this is the city's leading venue for operas and ballets. Some operas are sung in Bulgarian and some in Italian,

ALEXANDER NEVSKY SQUARE MARKET

A not-to-be-missed open-air market selling World War II and Communist-era memorabilia, stamps, postcards, coins, medals and assorted bric-a-brac. Very little schlock, apart from the cheaply lacquered Russian dolls and the array of reproduction icons. Cross the square to the eastern side for women selling embroidered lace, cardigans and tablecloths. ⓐ Alexander Nevsky Sq, north of Alexander Nevsky Memorial Church
🕐 09.00–18.00

◔ The Alexander Nevsky Square Market

⬤ *Mirella Bratova Workshop at Tsar Shishman Street*

so check beforehand to find out what's being staged. ⓐ Vrabcha St 1
ⓣ (02) 987 1366 ⓦ www.operasofia.bg ⓛ 09.30–18.30 Mon–Fri,
10.30–18.00 Sat & Sun

RETAIL THERAPY

Art Gallery Paris This small, owner-run gallery sells original work
by a new generation of unknown Bulgarian artists specialising
in figurative and expressive art. Parizh Street runs along the west
side of Alexander Nevsky Memorial Church and the shop is near
the National Opera House. ⓐ Parizh St 8 ⓣ (02) 980 8093
ⓦ www.gallery-paris.com ⓛ 11.00–14.00, 14.30–18.30 Mon–Fri,
11.00–14.00 Sat

Casyopea A natural cosmetics store selling exotic handmade soaps,
body oils and butters, bath minerals and salts, and other spa products.
ⓐ Tsar Shishman St 19 ⓣ (02) 980 4652 ⓦ www.casyopea.com
ⓛ 10.00–20.00 Mon–Sat

Cheers Three outlets in this part of the city with good selections of
Bulgarian wines and spirits. ⓐ Vasil Levski Blvd 59 ⓣ (02) 987 1252;
ⓐ Tsar Osvoboditel Blvd 14 ⓣ (02) 986 1856; ⓐ Rakovski St 116
ⓣ (02) 981 2729 ⓦ www.cheers.bg ⓛ 09.00–22.00 Mon–Sat,
10.00–21.00 Sun

Grita Gallery Alongside the paintings in which this gallery majors,
you'll see many an item of sculpture and other, more esoteric, forms
of art. It's always worth a visit as turnover is high, and you never
know what delights will be sitting coyly in the window. ⓐ Vrabcha
St 14 ⓣ 0887 769392 ⓛ 10.30–19.00 Mon–Fri, 11.00–17.00 Sat

Mirella Bratova Workshop Bratova, the designer who makes the clothes you see in this one-off boutique, works with linen and silk to produce trousers, jackets and suits for women and some lovely tops using Thai silk. One of the more original designers in Sofia. ⓐ Tsar Shishman St 4 ⓣ (02) 980 7156 ⓦ www.mirellabratova.com ⓛ 10.30–20.00 Mon–Fri, 10.30–18.00 Sat

Noe Gallery Original Bulgarian artwork – paintings, wood and bronze carvings – of some quality. You could engage in a little gentle bargaining, though prices are reasonable. ⓐ Vrabcha St 12A ⓣ (02) 980 6941 ⓦ www.gallerynoe.com ⓛ 12.00–18.30 Mon–Sat

Pretty Things Workshop A delightful shop offering a wide range of beautiful handmade souvenirs, gifts, home decorations and bedding. ⓐ Krakra St 12 ⓣ (02) 943 8220 ⓦ www.pretty-things-workshop.com ⓛ 10.00–20.00 Mon–Fri, 11.00–18.00 Sat

TAKING A BREAK

Devette Drakona £ ❶ An essential for fans of Chinese food, with wonderful views of the magnificent Russian Church of St Nicholas across the street. ⓐ Tsar Osvoboditel Blvd 8A ⓣ (02) 981 8878 ⓛ 11.30–23.30

Mamma Mia £ ❷ Cheap and cheerful pasta and pizza restaurant with upstairs tables on a terrace; the tables on your left as you enter the courtyard belong to the cosy Mediterrani bar, which is under its own management. ⓐ Tsar Shishman St 39 ⓣ (02) 981 2727 ⓛ 10.00–00.00

Onda £ ❸ A very Western-style joint where latte-sipping café habitués will feel at home. Cookies, muffins and sandwiches are on the menu and, upstairs, more fine views of the Russian Church. Wireless internet connection is available here. ⓐ Tsar Osvoboditel Blvd 8 ⓣ (02) 987 4920 ⓦ www.onda.bg ⓛ 07.00–21.00

AFTER DARK

RESTAURANTS

Victoria £ ❹ This is a fabulous restaurant with delicious thin crispy pizzas, a great selection of pasta dishes, and luxuriant fresh salads. Its back garden overlooking Alexander Nevsky Square is delightful in summer. The menu also offers a wide range of wines. ⓐ Tsar Osvoboditel Blvd 7 ⓣ (02) 986 ⓦ www.victoria.bg ⓛ 24 hrs

Bibliotekata ££ ❺ There's nothing academic about this Japanese sushi bar and adjoining piano bar and retro live music club in the basement of the National Library. Over a dozen choices of sushi and plenty of main dishes along the lines of scallop with cream, spicy sauce, teriyaki chicken, beef teppanyaki and a dessert of ice cream tempura. ⓐ Vasil Levski Blvd 88 ⓣ (02) 943 4004 ⓛ Sushi bar: 11.30–01.00; bar/club: 21.00–04.00

Egur, Egur ££ ❻ Armenian restaurant where the wallpaper, varnished wood flooring and (unplayed) piano create a homely and comfortable mood. Appetising starters like the Armenian sausages or *shtoratz* (fried aubergine rolls), followed by mostly meat-based dishes like *massis* (chicken stuffed with salmon and spinach) with a choice of tasty garnishes. ⓐ Dobrudzha St 10 ⓣ (02) 989 3383 ⓛ 11.00–23.30

Mahaloto ££ ❼ Mahaloto (Bulgarian for 'pendulum') is rather special because it creates an intimate restaurant atmosphere without sacrificing the need for carefully prepared meals and good service. There are familiar Bulgarian dishes on the menu but the more Western dishes are equally good – a rare achievement – and there is a decent wine list (though no cocktails). A brick cellar setting but tables also outside in the summer. ⓐ Vasil Levski Blvd 51 ⓣ (02) 980 3085 ⓛ 11.00–00.00

Checkpoint Charly £££ ❽ The name refers to the crossing point on the Berlin Wall, and the Cold War theme is playfully persistent in this stylish restaurant – the placemats reproduce Bulgaria's old Communist newspaper. At weekends a live jazz band performs. The food is international and receives good reviews. ⓐ Ivan Vazov St 12 ⓣ (02) 988 0370 ⓛ 10.00–00.30 Sun–Thur, 10.00–02.00 Fri & Sat

Krim £££ ❾ The most stately of Sofia's restaurants, set in and outside a 19th-century grand house, and one of the few that has survived from the Communist era. Bulgarian, Russian and fish dishes. ⓐ Slavyanska St 17 ⓣ (02) 988 6950 ⓦ www.krim.bg ⓛ 12.00–00.00

Uno Enoteca £££ ❿ One of Sofia's very best and most European restaurants. Come here for an atmosphere of subdued elegance. Starters include Parma ham with melon, foie gras or a Caesar salad, and the choice of dishes will satisfy carnivores and vegetarians. An exemplary wine list and impeccable service. ⓐ Vasil Levski Blvd 45 ⓣ (02) 981 4372 ⓦ www.uno-sofia.com ⓛ 10.00–01.00

NIGHTLIFE

Motto Lively, trendy bar and diner with a modern interior, huge drinks menu, selection of light snacks and Wi-Fi access. Very popular with young locals. ⓐ Aksakov St 18 ⓣ (02) 987 2723 ⓦ www.motto-bg.com ⓒ 10.00–01.00

My Mojito Dark and cosy club with two DJs spinning soft and soothing sounds in separate rooms – a relaxed watering hole for Sofia's sophisticated young ones; a good list of cocktails and a sociable atmosphere. ⓐ Ivan Vazov Street 12 ⓣ 0895 490 691 ⓒ 21.00–05.00

Planet Club There are raucous DJ parties every night, but you can also go during the day to have coffee, lunch or an early evening drink gazing at photos from old films and musical instruments on the walls. Just behind the Alexander Nevsky Memorial Church. ⓐ Oborishte St 1A ⓣ (02) 981 3532 ⓒ 09.00–04.00

Yalta Very close to the Radisson Blu Grand Hotel, this is one of the hot spots in Sofia's club scene and regularly hosts famous international DJs. Stylish modern interior and plenty of beautiful young creatures. ⓐ Tsar Osvoboditel Blvd 20 ⓣ 0897 870 230 ⓦ www.yaltaclub.com ⓒ 20.00–06.00

Around Vitosha Boulevard

Vitosha Boulevard begins at the southern side of Sveta Nedelya Square and stretches south in a long straight line as if heading directly for Mount Vitosha (see page 116), which looms attractively in the distance. Once filled with traffic, Vitosha Boulevard is now barred to vehicles except for the clunking trams that trundle up and down, lending a pleasantly old-fashioned feel to the broad street.

The mostly featureless buildings that line each side of the boulevard have been converted at street level into upmarket shops, and Vitosha Boulevard is now the premier shopping area for city residents; the all-too-familiar brand names and logos help to make it the most European-looking part of Sofia. The triumph of consumerism in this area leaves little space for cultural attractions, although the boulevard does lead to the National Palace of Culture (see page 95) and a large green area devoted to rest and relaxation.

SIGHTS & ATTRACTIONS

Monument to the Bulgarian State

As you enter NDK Garden at the junction of Vitosha Boulevard and Patriarh Evtimii Boulevard, look for what resembles a grotesquely vandalised structure. This hideous metal agglomeration is the Monument to the Bulgarian State, built in 1981 to mark the thirteen hundred years anniversary of AD 681 when Han Asparuh led the Bulgars into what is now Bulgaria. What you see is a strong contender for the ugliest example of Soviet-era public art anywhere in the world.
❸ Northern end of NDK Garden

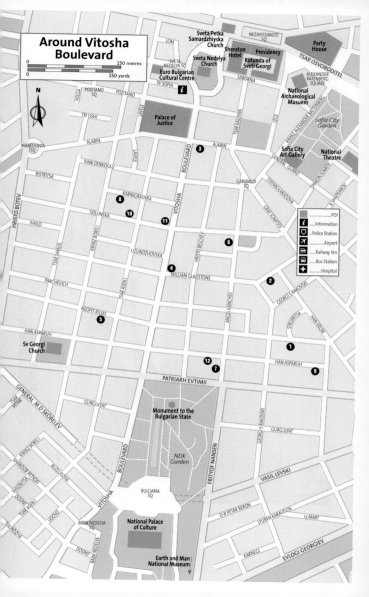

⬤ *The Monument to the Bulgarian State*

CULTURE

Earth and Man National Museum

Here you'll find literally thousands of exhibits of minerals, giant crystals and precious stones. The museum also hosts chamber concerts and all sorts of other cultural and charity events. ⓐ Cherni Vrah Blvd 4 (behind Hilton Hotel) ⓣ (02) 865 6639 ⓦ www.earthandman.org ⓛ 10.00–18.00 Tues–Sat ⓝ Tram: 6. Admission charge

National Palace of Culture

Usually referred to as NDK, this monstrous edifice was constructed in 1981 to celebrate the country's 13th centenary, although it now

NDK GARDEN

This is the most popular park for the city's youth, and every evening and weekend the place is like a magnet for teenagers who hang out here with their skateboards or simply sit and dangle their legs over the concrete parapets – the pedestrian bridge that leads from behind the NDK towards the Hilton Hotel is a favourite spot for romantically inclined couples. There are kiosks selling candyfloss and drinks, and just before the pedestrian bridge a bar with outdoor aluminium seating where a drink and a snack can be enjoyed in the daytime or at night. It is only on the other side of the Hilton that actual greenery makes an appearance and even then it has a fairly unkempt look that tends to put you off wandering through it. ⓐ Between Vitosha Blvd & Frityof Nansen Blvd, beginning on corner of Patriarh Evtimii Blvd ⓝ Tram: 1, 7

seems only to celebrate the worst excesses of unimaginative architects who worked for the government in the Communist era. It houses concert halls, an exhibition space and shops.

a Bulgaria Sq 1 t (02) 916 6360 w www.ndk.bg l 09.00–19.00
Tram: 1, 7

RETAIL THERAPY

Art Alley Gallery Bulgarian and international art for sale, based around exhibitions that tend to change every month or so, with any

● *National Palace of Culture (NDK)*

necessary packing arranged by the shop. From Vitosha Boulevard, turn into William Gladstone Street and cross two blocks; the shop is on your right just after crossing Angel Kanchev Street at the end of the second block. ⓐ William Gladstone St 51A ☏ (02) 986 7363 🕒 10.30–20.00 Tues–Fri, 11.00–19.00 Sat & Sun

Bitsiani A men's fashion store selling snazzy jackets, shirts and ties as well as shoes and sportswear. ⓐ Vitosha Blvd 32 ☏ (02) 989 7409 🕒 10.00–20.00 Mon–Sat

Booktrading The best bookshop for English-language material, including hiking maps of Mount Vitosha. ⓐ Vitosha Blvd 9 ⓣ 0894 770 234 ⓦ www.booktrading.bg ⓛ 09.30–21.00

Dar Za Gorene An Aladdin's cave of colourful candles: shelf upon shelf of unique handmade candles inspired by traditional Bulgarian motifs, with symbols for harmony, love, nature and beauty. ⓐ Frityof Nansen Blvd 19 ⓣ 0888 647 516 ⓦ www.darzagorene.com ⓛ 10.00–20.00 Mon–Fri

Orange Multimedia store with four floors of stationery, toys, Bulgarian and foreign books and a broad selection of CDs, DVDs and games. There are copying and printing services in the basement and a nice restaurant on the fifth floor where you can stop for a cup of coffee. ⓐ Graf Ignatiev St 18 ⓣ (02) 981 0400 ⓛ 09.00–21.00 Mon–Fri, 10.00–20.00 Sat & Sun

TAKING A BREAK

Apartment £ ❶ This really is an apartment in a 19th-century building, where the spacious, high-ceilinged rooms are decorated with quirky furnishings and artworks. Serves healthy juices and teas as well as exotic vegetarian dishes and desserts. ⓐ Neofit Rilski St 68 ⓣ 0896 652 087 ⓛ 12.00–01.00

Divaka £ ❷ Just near Slaveykov Square you can sample simple but hearty Bulgarian cuisine. The menu may not be extensive, but everything on it is tasty, fresh and inexpensive. ⓐ William Gladstone St 54 ⓣ (02) 989 9543 ⓛ 24 hrs

● Sveta Sofia statue on Vitosha Boulevard

Dream House £ ❸ Look for a sign for the entrance to the Internet Hostel, open the white door on the left and walk up the staircase to reach this vegetarian restaurant. Snack on starters like vegetable sushi in a spicy sauce with an avocado salad or make a meal of it with tofu and rice in sweet and sour sauce, or grilled courgette and tahini sauce. An eatery during the day but more restaurant-like at night; a buffet all day Sunday. Good drinks list. ⓐ Alabin St 50A ⓣ (02) 980 8163 ⓛ 11.30–22.00

Ugo £ ❹ Reasonable pizzas plus reasonable prices plus a great atmosphere equals very popular. If it's late or you're feeling lazy, get the pizza delivered to your hotel. ⓐ Vitosha Blvd 45 ⓣ Restaurant: (02) 986 4809; delivery: (02) 986 4000 ⓛ 24 hrs

Villa Rosiche £ ❺ Look for a blue plaque on the wall outside, and if you find yourself passing the Niky Hotel, you've missed it. Tucked away in a quiet courtyard, this is a neat little hideaway from the hubbub of Vitosha Boulevard. Cakes and chocolate truffles, coffees and a tempting choice of croissants, including ones stuffed with mozzarella and tomato or brie and broccoli. Cocktails and fruit drinks, with outdoor tables in the shade. ⓐ Neofit Rilski St 26 ⓣ (02) 954 3072 ⓛ 08.00–21.00

AFTER DARK

RESTAURANTS

Dani's £ ❻ Excellent little deli-café, ideal for a lunch break on a warm day when the homemade lemonade goes down a treat with a salad, soup and sandwich. ⓐ Angel Kanchev 18A ⓣ (02) 980 4548 ⓦ www.bistrodanis.com ⓛ 10.00–22.00

◆ *Enjoy sweet pastries at Villa Rosiche*

The Fox & Hound ££ ❼ Aha! A traditional pub atmosphere. The menu includes classical Bulgarian dishes as well as a wide range of European food. It's worth trying broccoli and blue cheese soup, or lamb meatballs with spinach, if you fancy a pub lunch with a difference. ⓐ Angel Kanchev St 34 ❶ (02) 980 7427 ⓦ www.foxandhound.bg ❶ 10.00–00.00

J.J. Murphy's ££ ❽ All too familiar Irish-themed pub in some respects, but reassuring when it comes to delivering a decent pint of Murphy's and recognisable dishes like shepherd's pie. This is also the best place to be sure of catching a satellite-transmitted football match. ⓐ Karnigradska St 6 ❶ (02) 980 2870 ⓦ www.jjmurphys.com ❶ 12.00–00.00

Manastirska Magernitsa ££ ❾ A contender for that last night in the city when you want a leisurely dining experience and a reminder that you are well and truly in the Balkans. The setting is perfect – a 19th-century house decorated in traditional Bulgarian style – for a menu of time-honoured dishes from the country's many monasteries. ⓐ Han Asparuh St 67 ❶ (02) 980 3883 ⓦ www.magernitsa.com ❶ 11.00–00.00

Pri Yafata ££ ❿ A good place to start satisfying your curiosity about Bulgarian cuisine because the grilled meats and salads are authentic national favourites. The décor looks kitschy but is actually genuine. ⓐ Solunska St 28 ❶ (02) 980 1727 ❶ 10.00–01.00

Upstairs ££ ⓫ Fashionable diner with metal chairs on a narrow balcony overlooking Sofia's main drag, and tables and sofas in the arty interior. You can turn up for just drinks and enjoy the scene or tuck into the salads, pasta or dishes like chicken satay and pineapple. Coffees include a Drambuie-topped 'Prince Charles' ('for refined gentlemen') and plenty of cocktails. ⓐ Vitosha Blvd 18 ⓣ (02) 989 9696 ⓛ 10.00–02.00 summer; 10.00–00.00 winter

Da Vidi £££ ⓬ The minimalist style and floor-to-ceiling windows may be a familiar format in other European cities, but this is hip stuff for Sofia and makes for an agreeable night out. The continental-style food is well-prepared with excellent fish dishes, and the wine list goes well beyond the national confines. ⓐ Han Asparuh St 36 ⓣ (02) 980 6746 ⓛ 10.00–23.00

NIGHTLIFE

Escape Escape is Sofia's number-one nightclub, where techno and house music is belted out from the top-notch sound system. High-flying DJs are part of the attraction. Sophisticated in many respects, and it rightly brags about Jean-Claude Van Damme turning up here one night. ⓐ Angel Kanchev St 1 ⓣ 0889 990000 ⓦ www.clubescape.bg ⓛ 22.00–04.00 Thur–Sat. Admission charge

Life House A trendy club with stylish and modern design that whacks out house music. ⓐ Vitosha Blvd 12 ⓣ 0888 241016 ⓦ www.clublifehouse.com ⓛ 22.00–06.00. Admission charge

Outside the centre

Sofia's most significant cultural attractions, the medieval frescoes at Boyana Church and the National History Museum, are located 8 km (5 miles) southwest of the city centre in the affluent suburb of Boyana. It is a 20-minute ride by taxi but takes over an hour by public transport.

If you decide to take public transport to Boyana Church, catch tram 9 on Makedonia Square, a five-minute walk from Sveta Nedelya Square, to its terminus at Hladilnika. Then walk through the tiny market of wooden stalls – just follow fellow passengers – to a street with lots of bus stops. Turn left and walk to an open area with more bus stops, and look for the one indicating bus 64, which goes past Boyana Church.

To reach the National History Museum, take tram 5 from Makedonia Square to Totleben Boulevard, then catch bus 63. Alternatively, take trolleybus 2 from outside Sofia University to its terminus and then walk across the main street and turn left to reach the museum.

The other sights and attractions in this chapter are only a five- or ten-minute walk from Alexander Nevsky Memorial Church and so can be reached on foot or by a short taxi ride.

SIGHTS & ATTRACTIONS

Borisova Gradina

From the Soviet Army Monument, it is a minute's walk to the entrance of the city's most spacious and attractive park and two stadiums. Renamed Borisova Gradina (Boris Garden) after 1989, it is still widely known as Freedom Park – a name associated with the Communist era and officially discarded for this reason. Developed and perfected by three successive gardeners, the park is large enough never to feel

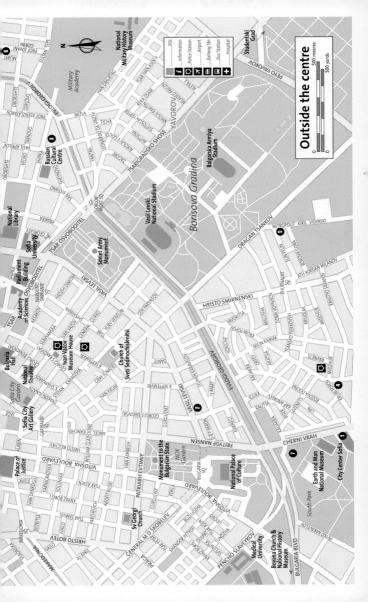

crowded, and joggers have the footpaths to themselves early in the morning. Ideal for picnics on a warm day. ⓐ South of Orlov Most ⓛ 24 hrs

Soviet Army Monument

From Narodno Sabranie Square, Tsar Osvoboditel Boulevard heads towards Orlov Most (Eagles' Bridge), which crosses the puny River Perlovska. The bridge marks the spot where returning Bulgarian prisoners of war, released from Ottoman prisons after liberation in 1878, were greeted rapturously by their fellow citizens. The prisoners were christened 'the eagles', hence the creatures adorning the bridge on each side.

Before reaching the bridge, you will see the Soviet Army Monument, erected in 1954 to acknowledge the liberation of the country from Nazi submission (see page 14). These days, skateboarders hone their skills around the monument, seemingly oblivious to their own history. ⓐ Tsar Osvoboditel Blvd near Orlov Most

CULTURE

Boyana Church

The work of anonymous 13th-century artists, the church frescoes are Bulgaria's most important contribution to medieval European culture – not least because they are so well preserved and complete – and careful restoration work shows just how astonishing the artists' achievement was. Art historians compare their mastery of pictorial realism, use of the vernacular and mature awareness of colour to the achievement of Giotto (who was not even born when work began on these frescoes), founder of the Florentine school of painting and harbinger of the Italian Renaissance. How influential the Boyana

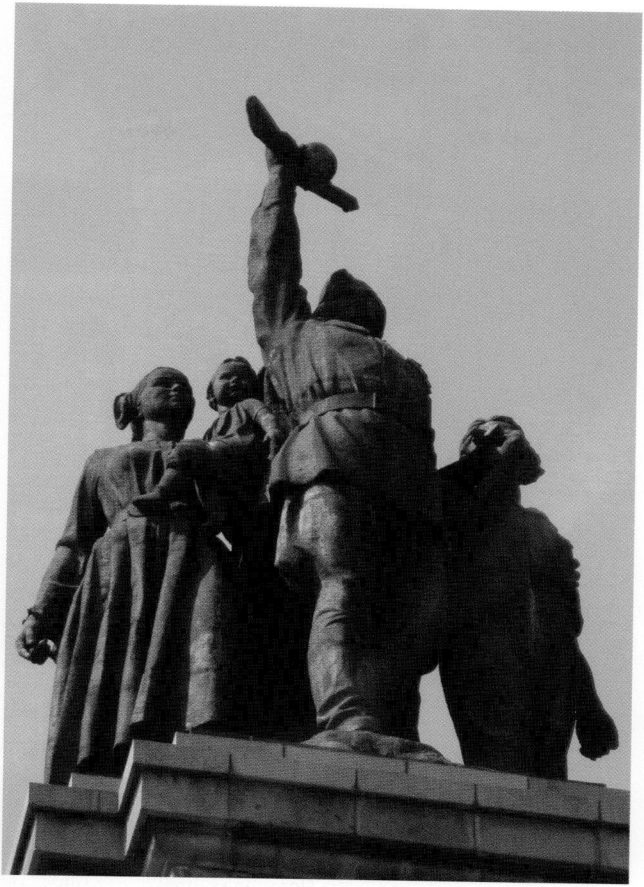

The Soviet Army Monument

Rear view of the ancient Boyana Church

artists were in the development of Western European painting is a subject of debate, though there is no disputing their effect on mural painting in Russia and Eastern Europe. Although the frescoes pay homage to the canon of medieval icon painting and the traditions of Byzantine art, there is no mistaking the innovatory display of individuality and celebration of ordinary life in the more than 240 figures that populate the frescoes.

Visitor numbers and their time inside the church are strictly limited, and to study the frescoes in detail you will need to visit the nearby church museum where reproductions are on display. Boyana Church is a UNESCO World Heritage Site. ⓐ Boyansko Ezero St 1–3, Boyana ⓣ (02) 959 0939 ⓦ www.boyanachurch.org ⓛ 09.30–17.30 Apr–Oct; 09.00–17.00 Nov–Mar ⓝ See page 104. Admission charge

National History Museum

The city and the country's most prestigious museum, once located in the heart of the city, was moved to the suburb of Boyana to make use of a grand palatial building once used by the Communist government. What you will see here is an engaging ethnographic exhibition on the top floor, assorted artefacts from the ancient times and the Middle Ages, and a collection of frescoes from monasteries around the country. ⓐ Vitoshko Lale 16, Boyana ⓣ (02) 955 4280 ⓦ www.historymuseum.org ⓛ 09.30–18.00 Apr–Oct; 09.00–17.30 Nov–Mar ⓝ See page 104. Admission charge (combined ticket for museum and Boyana Church available. There is a separate charge if you wish to use a camera.)

National Military History Museum

The paraphernalia in the cabinets inside the museum – uniforms, weapons and the like – will tend to appeal only to military buffs,

PATRON OF THE ARTS

In 1259, Sevastocrator Kaloyan expanded the church at Boyana and commissioned a group of artists – their names lost to posterity – to illuminate the interior with frescoes. One of the finest paintings you will see in Boyana depicts Kaloyan in the contemporary dress of nobles holding a model of the church in his hands alongside his wife, Desislava.

but the hardware on show outside is the real draw. There are MiG jet fighters, missile launchers and SS23 missiles from the Soviet era alongside the phenomenally versatile Russian T34 tank that played a crucial role in the defeat of German forces by the USSR. ❷ Cherkovna St 92 ❶ (02) 946 1805 Ⓦ www.militarymuseum.bg Ⓛ 10.00–18.00 Wed–Sun Ⓝ Tram: 20. Admission charge

RETAIL THERAPY

Carpet House Authentic Chiprovtsi kilims, hand-woven with traditional Bulgarian designs of brightly coloured geometrical figures. They are made of natural materials (wool and plant-based dyes) and last over 30 years. ❷ Rakovski St 38 ❶ (02) 983 6609 Ⓦ www.tchukilim.com Ⓛ 10.00–19.00 Mon–Fri, 10.00–14.00 Sat Ⓝ Trolleybus: 9

City Center Sofia Huge complex with over 100 shops such as Marks & Spencer, Guy Laroche, Calvin Klein, Bata and Nike. There's also a buzzing fast-food area, several cafés and a Cineplex, with six cinema halls. ❷ Arsenalski Blvd 2 ❶ (02) 865 7285 Ⓦ www.ccs-mall.com Ⓛ 10.00–22.00 Ⓝ Tram: 6

TAKING A BREAK

There is a small café inside the National History Museum, a touristy restaurant called Boyansko Hanche right near the Boyana Church bus station, and several cheaper (and better) eateries dotted about the area.

Fancy £ ❶ With its lively atmosphere, friendly and informal service and great variety of European food, this is the perfect place for a break in your shopping tour. ⓐ Arsenalski Blvd 2, City Center Sofia ❶ (02) 963 4480 Ⓦ www.fancybg.com Ⓛ 10.00–00.00 Ⓝ Tram: 6

Fix Mix £ ❷ Big on cocktails, with at least 40 available, alongside salmon sandwiches and other tasty snacks. It's decorated in fruity colours, with light, modern furniture and funky music. ⓐ Vasil Levski

🔺 *Pretty handicrafts make perfect souvenirs*

Blvd 24 ☎ (02) 987 3171 ⓦ www.fixmix-culture.com ⏰ 08.00–22.00
Mon–Fri, 10.00–22.00 Sat & Sun ⓝ 5-min walk from NDK

O! Shipka £ ❸ Well worth seeking out for an inexpensive but tasty
pizza, salad or Mexican-style dish. Tables inside, where sociability
raises the noise level, or a pleasant garden setting, where peace and
quiet can be enjoyed and a glass of wine or two sipped contentedly.
ⓐ Shipka St 11 ☎ (02) 944 9288 ⓦ www.oshipka.bg ⏰ 24 hrs
ⓝ Tram: 1, 7

AFTER DARK

RESTAURANTS
Arkadia ££ ❹ Hidden away down a quiet street – walking down
Sveti Naum from the Hilton end, take the second left, but if you
reach the Lotenetz Hotel you have gone past the turning – this
restaurant and bar is not known to many visitors and it makes for
a perfect getaway and a quiet meal. The menu features a variety
of starters, more than half a dozen vegetarian dishes, fondue

STUDENTSKI GRAD
Studentski Grad, 'student city', is a suburb 7 km (4⅓ miles)
southeast of the city centre and home to 10,000 bright young
people intent on having a good time when not inside a lecture
theatre. There are countless bars and pubs, and the neighbourhood
can be reached by taking a bus from Shipka Street to the end
of the line. You will need a taxi to get back to town but they
are easy to find around the bars. ⓝ Bus: 94, 280

(Bulgarian style) and all sorts of meats. Eat inside, downstairs (where there is a snooker table and dartboard) or outside. A good list of Bulgarian wines. ⓐ Krum Popov St 64 ❶ (02) 865 8484 ❷ 11.00–00.00 ❸ Tram: 6

Pod Lipite ££ ❺ At the southwest side of Borisova Gradina, this restaurant is a must. Decorated in traditional Bulgarian style and featuring live folk music in the evenings, this is the perfect place to taste genuine meals prepared from old Bulgarian recipes. If it sounds like touristy kitsch, it is – but that's all part of the fun. ⓐ Elin Pelin St 5 ❶ (02) 866 5053 ❿ www.podlipitebg.com ❷ 12.00–01.00 ❸ Tram: 9, 18; metro: Vasil Levski National Stadium

Pri Miro ££ ❻ Either a fairly long walk from the centre of town or a short taxi ride is justified in order to experience this authentic Serbian restaurant. Bulgarians and Serbs share a love of grilled meats, and this is the place to taste the differences in style and taste. The firm favourites are the *pleskavice* (sausage-like patties of minced meat) and *cevapcici* (rissoles), and there are some very tasty relishes to go with either. One of Sofia's best restaurants. ⓐ Murfi St 34 ❶ (02) 943 7127 ❷ 12.00–00.00 ❸ Tram: 20

Seasons £££ ❼ Seasons has the best themed buffets in the city and Mondays, devoted to Bulgarian cuisine, provide an excellent introduction to the country's food. There is also an à la carte menu and, in the summer, tables on the terrace with views of Mount Vitosha. ⓐ Hilton Hotel, Bulgaria Blvd 1 ❶ (02) 933 5062 ❷ 06.30–23.30 ❸ Tram: 6

NIGHTLIFE

Bar Na Kraia Na Vselenata In English, this is named the 'Bar at the End of the Universe' and describes itself as themed around 'the fragmented remains of an eventually ruined planet, which is enclosed in a vast time bubble and projected forward in time to the precise moment of The End of The Universe'. Very Douglas Adams! What you actually get is a large circular bar and brightly painted walls, plus a lively scene with a friendly atmosphere and a long list of cocktails. 🄰 Studentski Grad, Block 34, next to Entrance B 🄣 (02) 962 5541 🄲 09.00–02.00 🄽 Bus: 94, 280

Marseille A café-club with a good reputation for party nights, especially at weekends, playing retro, latino, pop and rock. 🄰 Prof. Dr Ivan Stranski St 5, Studentski Grad, between Blocks 55 and 56 🄣 (02) 968 1977 🄲 08.00–02.00 🄽 Bus: 94, 280

Swingin' Hall The best place in Sofia for everyone who likes live rock, pop and jazz performances, and it has two stages for alternating bands. 🄰 Dragan Tsankov Blvd 8 🄣 (02) 963 0696 🄲 21.00–04.00 Tues–Sun 🄽 Tram: 9, 18; metro: Vasil Levski National Stadium. Admission charge

Toucan Bluzz & Rock A pub that serves up live rock and blues. It also does the best karaoke in Sofia every Thursday night. 🄰 Akademik Boris Stefanov St 4, Studentski Grad 🄣 0887 098164 🄲 21.00–04.00 🄽 Bus: 94, 280

▶ *Traditional houses in Blagoevgrad's Varosha district*

OUT OF TOWN
trips

Mount Vitosha

Mount Vitosha is clearly visible from Sofia's city centre, and it only takes a 7 km (just over 4 miles) bus ride to reach the foothills of this 2,290 m (7,513 ft) outcrop of rock and pine forests. You can visit Mount Vitosha all year round, and whether skiing or hiking the best place to start off is Aleko (see page 118). There are a number of marked trails through the woods and, outside winter, a day out with a picnic suggests itself as an ideal excursion from the city. You can either take a bus to Dragalevtsi (see page 118) and walk to a chairlift to Aleko, or take the bus to Simeonovo (see page 120) for a cable car to Aleko.

GETTING THERE

Hladilnika bus station, the one used to reach Boyana (see page 104), serves the Mount Vitosha area. To reach the station, take tram 9 from either Makedonia Square or from Slaveykov Square or Alabin Street, both a five-minute walk from Sveta Nedelya Square, to its terminus at Hladilnika. Walk through the small market of wooden stalls beside the tram lines onto a street full of bus stops. Turn left and walk to an open area with more bus stops.

Bus 64 goes to Dragalevtsi and Boyana villages; bus 93 goes through the village and on to the chairlift; bus 98 goes to Dragalevtsi and to Simeonovo village; bus 122 goes to the Simeonovo cable car. You can use your usual tram tickets on these routes. Check return times of buses at the kiosk or ask the driver.

To get to Aleko from either village, you can either take the chairlift (from Dragalevtsi, see page 118) or cable car (from Simeonovo, see page 120), or hire a taxi.

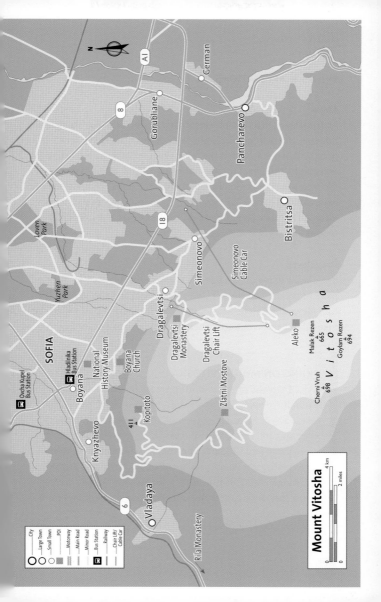

Mount Vitosha

N

A1

German

8

Gorubliane

Pancharevo

18

Bistritsa

Loven Park

Simeonovo

Yuzhen Park

Simeonovo Cable Car

Dragalevtsi

V i t o s h a

SOFIA

Ovcha Kupel Bus Station

Hadlinika Bus Station

National History Museum

Boyana Church

Dragalevtsi Monastery

Dragalevtsi Chair Lift

Aleko

Malak Rezen 665

Boyana

Kopitoto

Zlatni Mostove

Chemi Vruh 698

Goylam Rezen 694

Knyazhevo

411

6

Vladaya

Rila Monastery

◯	City
◯	Large Town
◯	Small Town
■	POI
	Motorway
	Main Road
	Minor Road
	Railway
◼	Bus Station
	Chair Lift/ Cable Car

0 ___ 4 km
0 ___ 2 miles

SIGHTS & ATTRACTIONS

Aleko

Aleko styles itself as a winter resort and a base for skiing. Skiing apart, however, visitor infrastructure is fairly decrepit. There is a functioning hotel with a restaurant at the point where the Dragalevtsi chair lift ends, and although plans are in the pipeline for a new, 5-star hotel in the resort, that is currently about it. From the hotel, it is a five-minute walk to the ski slopes. In summer, it takes less than an hour for an invigorating walk up to Cherni Vruh (Black Peak), the summit of Mount Vitosha.

Dragalevtsi

If you want to get off the bus at Dragalevtsi village, look for a lemon-painted building on the left side of the street and the cobbled Tsar Ivan Alexander Square. The journey from Hladilnika bus station only takes about seven minutes. There are hotels with restaurants in

SKIING ON MOUNT VITOSHA

Mount Vitosha offers around 29 km (18 miles) of ski runs suitable for beginners and more advanced skiers. The season lasts from late December through to early April, although the start and end times vary from year to year. In the ski base of Aleko you'll find the **Ski & Snowboard School Aleko Moten** (❶ (02) 967 1141), where you can hire equipment and English-speaking instructors (the latter with 24-hour notice). There is also a special ski run for night skiing, open on weekdays from 18.00–22.00.

● *Snow-capped Mount Vitosha*

Dragalevtsi, and from here it takes about 40 minutes to walk up to the chairlift. Facing the square from the bus stop, take the road that begins in the top right corner of the square and, after about half an hour, turn left off the road where a sign points to the Vodenitzata restaurant. The chairlift is less than ten minutes away up this road, and it stops at a mid-way station on its way up to Aleko. ❶ Chairlift: (02) 967 1110 🕒 09.00–17.00 Thur–Sun, summer; 09.00–16.00 Tues–Sun, winter

Simeonovo

The village of Simeonovo is less attractive than Dragalevtsi (which itself is not especially eye-catching) and, with fewer amenities by way of places to eat, the only reason to come here would be to take the cable car up to Aleko. ❶ Cable car: (02) 961 2189 🕒 09.00–18.00 Fri–Sun, summer; 09.00–16.30 Tues–Sun, winter

Zlatni Mostove

Zlatni Mostove (Golden Bridges) is an attractive area of evergreen forest and the misleadingly named Stone River, which is not really a river but a dramatic series of huge boulders deposited at the end of the last ice age under which flows a paltry stream. There are a number of marked hiking routes and, if you are making a day of it, take the one to Cherni Vruh, the peak of Mount Vitosha. It takes almost three hours, so be sure to bring water and food because there are no restaurants along the way. What you do get is a mildly spectacular landscape of peat bog. ❹ Accessible by car or taxi only; if travelling by taxi, arrange pick-up at an agreed time or take a mobile phone and a list of taxi numbers

▶ *The Stone River at Zlatni Mostove*

TAKING A BREAK

Helis Bar & Diner £ One of the coolest places in Dragalevtsi, with simple but perfect meals, a big TV screen and very friendly staff who create a homely and informal atmosphere. In the summer you can enjoy the panoramic view over Sofia. ⓐ Nartsis St 6, Dragalevtsi ⓣ (0895) 708 010 ⓛ 09.00–23.30

Lyutite Chushki £–££ The menu features a full range of salads and other cold dishes like smoked salmon or shrimp cocktail, and many lunchtime meals such as chicken bites with bacon, aubergine pastry and meat rolls. Pork, chicken and fish meals are also available. To find the restaurant, keep the village square on your left and walk 200 m (219 yds) further along Krairechna Street, the road where the bus from Sofia stops, and it is on your right. ⓐ Krairechna St 26, Dragalevtsi ⓣ (02) 967 2220 ⓦ www.lutitechushki.com ⓛ 10.00–00.00

The Old House £–££ One of the most pleasant places to enjoy a meal in Dragalevtsi, and you will find it by taking the road that leads from the village square to the chairlift. It is on the left, less than five minutes from the village and, although the name is not in English, is easy to identify by its rustic-looking, alpine exterior. ⓐ General Kovatchev St 9, Dragalevtsi ⓣ (02) 967 2959 ⓛ 12.00–00.00

AFTER DARK

Hotel Darling Restaurant ££ Black caviar for starters, specialities such as fried trout and a host of chicken, veal and pork dishes help to make this restaurant well worth considering for an evening meal.

🄐 Yabalkova Gradina St 14, Dragalevtsi 📞 (02) 967 5018
🕐 10.00–00.00

Vodenitzata ££–£££ A folksy-looking, stone-built restaurant with
an attractive garden area. The food is traditional Bulgarian, and
evenings are enlivened by troupes of dancers in folk costumes.
It is best to make a reservation at weekends because large groups
can take over the place. 🄐 By the Dragalevtsi chairlift, Dragalevtsi
📞 (02) 967 1058 🌐 www.vodenitzata.com 🕐 12.00–00.00

ACCOMMODATION

Darling £ The second-best hotel in Dragalevtsi, with room rates
a little less than those of the Alexander Palace but with a better
restaurant (see Hotel Darling Restaurant opposite). 🄐 Yabalkova
Gradina St 14, Dragalevtsi 📞 (02) 967 5018 🌐 www.hotel-darling.com

Edi £ There are 14 inexpensive double rooms in this small but
basically comfortable hotel, and a restaurant on the first floor
as well as outdoor tables for food and drink. The Lyutite Chushki
restaurant (see opposite) is next door. 🄐 Krairechna St 28,
Dragalevtsi 📞 (02) 967 2270

Alexander Palace ££ Close to the village square, this is the best
hotel in Dragalevtsi in terms of amenities and general comfort.
Standard rooms have a fridge and there is little to be gained by
paying extra for one of the deluxe doubles. There is a restaurant
and sauna. 🄐 Nartsis St 1, Dragalevtsi 📞 (02) 967 1184
🌐 www.svetasofia-alexanders.com

Blagoevgrad

Two hours away by a regular bus service and 100 km (62 miles) south of Sofia, the university town of Blagoevgrad offers a day out to an animated and sophisticated city filled with bars, restaurants and a modicum of cultural attractions.

GETTING THERE

Regular buses (up to 20 per day) leave from Sofia's Central Bus Station (see page 53) and stop either in front of Blagoevgrad's railway station or at the bus terminal, just down the road. If you are dropped off at the bus terminal, walk out on to the street, turn left and walk the 200 m (219 yds) to the railway station and the junction. Turn right at the junction and walk up Bratya Miladinovi, past the Alen Mak Hotel to the main – and clearly identified – American University of Bulgaria. If you go to the right in front of the main building and cut through the small park, this will bring you into town and straight to the pavement tables outside the Pizza Napoli restaurant (see page 128). The centre of town is mostly pedestrianised, and the old part of town, Varosha, is on the other side of the small river and only a short walk away.

SIGHTS & ATTRACTIONS

Varosha

Varosha is the old quarter of the city, easy to reach on the other side of the river and readily identified by the cobbled streets and the traditional buildings that date back to the 19th century. Here you will find the Church of the Annunciation of the Virgin, its exterior

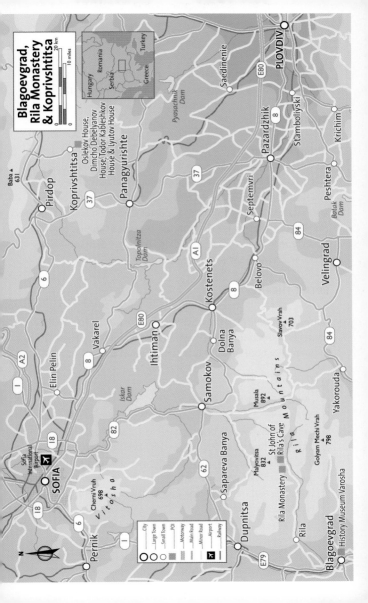

Blagoevgrad, Rila Monastery & Koprivshtitsa

Oslekov House, Dimcho Debelyanov House, Todor Kableshkov House & Lyutov House

Baba ▲ 631

0   10 miles
0   20 km

Hungary   Romania
Serbia   Greece   Turkey

PLOVDIV
Saedinenie
Pazardzhik
Stamboliyski
Krichim
Peshtera
Batak Dam
Velingrad
Yakorouda
History Museum Varosha
Blagoevgrad
Rila
Dupnitsa
Sapareva Banya
Samokov
Ihtiman
Vakarel
Elin Pelin
SOFIA
Sofia International Airport
Pernik
Koprivshtitsa
Pirdop
Panagyurishte
Kostenets
Dolna Banya
Belovo
Septemvri

Pyasachnik Dam
Topolnitsa Dam
Iskar Dam

Chemi Vrah 698
Vitosha

St John of Rila's Cave
Rila Monastery
Malyovitsa 832
Musala 892
Slavov Vrah 703
Golyam Mechi Vrah 798
Rila Mountains

E80
E79
A1
A2
37
6
8
18
82
62
84
1

City
Large Town
Small Town
POI
Motorway
Main Road
Minor Road
Airport
Railway

N

characterised by red and white stripes and murals decorating the portico. The folksy-looking Kristo Hotel is directly above the church.

CULTURE

History Museum

A motley collection of assorted finds from ancient times, religious artefacts in the form of icons and carvings, and outbursts of colour in a fine display of traditional costumes from the region. There is also a natural history section made up of stuffed birds and animals. None of the labelling is in English, but the cost of admission includes a brochure in English. ❸ Rila St 1 ❶ (073) 885 375 ⏱ 09.00–12.00, 13.00–18.00 Mon–Sat. Admission charge

RETAIL THERAPY

Mason Fairly typical of the small boutiques catering to the city's students and young people – cotton fabrics and funky, loose-fitting garments for both sexes. ❸ Bratya Kitanovi 10 ⏱ 11.00–19.30

AMERICAN UNIVERSITY

Blagoevgrad is a thriving university town thanks to the private American University of Bulgaria (AUBG), which was established in 1991 by the United States Agency for International Development (USAID) and the Bulgarian government. Teaching is entirely in English and students come from countries all over the region. It claims to have the largest English language library in southeastern Europe.

⬥ *The colourful façade of the Church of the Annunciation of the Virgin*

TAKING A BREAK

Kristal £ Always busy, with its outside tables dominating one corner of Macedonia Square, this is the place to sink into if you have an hour to spare to watch the world, well, Blagoevgrad, go by. ⓐ Macedonia Sq ❶ 0898 624 941 ❷ 08.30–00.00

Pizza Napoli £ One of the most popular pizza restaurants in town, on the central square just opposite the American University, with tables outside in the summer. Fresh salads, pizza and pasta, along with tasty meat dishes and a good choice of wines. ⓐ Hristo Botev Sq 4 ❶ (073) 882 388 ❷ 10.00–00.00

Varosha Restaurant £ Situated between the museum and the church in the old part of town, this timbered two-storey building blends in perfectly with the traditional ambience of the neighbourhood. The menu is unexciting but adequate for a lunch break, and there are two tables on a neat little balcony overlooking the river and park where you could happily while away the time with a drink. ⓐ Bistritsa St 10 ❶ (073) 881 370 ❷ 09.00–00.00

AFTER DARK

RESTAURANTS
Kristo £–££ On the first floor of the hotel and decked out in the traditional style that one would expect, this roomy restaurant has a menu that includes 40 different salads, hot and cold starters and grills. The dark wood décor gives the restaurant a rather sober atmosphere, and the best tables are those overlooking the cobbled

courtyard. ⓐ Kristo Hotel, Komitrov St, Varosha ① (073) 880 444
① 10.00–00.00

Dreams ££ Around the corner from Pizza Napoli and upstairs from
the Underground pub, this is the most formal restaurant in the city
in the evening. The menu is not in English but staff should be able
to translate; stick with the fish dishes because they're what they
do best. ⓐ Arseni Kostentsev St 7 ① (073) 834 526 ① 09.00–01.00

NIGHTLIFE
Underground This is the most popular nightspot in Blagoevgrad,
and the place is packed with students for the weekend discos.
There is also a separate bar but it is hard to escape the sound
system blasting out rock and pop-folk. ⓐ Arseni Kostentsev St 7
① (0899) 942211 ① 20.00–02.00

Vertigo No food but a long drinks list and lots of cocktails.
ⓐ Todor Alexandrov St 3 ① (073) 886 644 ① 24 hrs

ACCOMMODATION

Kristo £ This would be the first choice for any overnight stay in
Blagoevgrad. It is situated in the peaceful Varosha district but within
walking distance of the city's nightlife. There are over 30 rooms with
air-conditioning, a restaurant and bar (see opposite), and a sauna.
ⓐ Komitrov St, Varosha ① (073) 880 444 ⓦ www.hotelkristo.net

Rila Monastery

The Rila Mountains lie to the south of Mount Vitosha, but it takes longer to reach the famed Rila Monastery, 120 km (75 miles) from Sofia. Although a day trip from the capital is feasible, most visitors spend a night outside Sofia in order to make the journey a less hectic one.

GETTING THERE

There is only one bus directly to Rila Monastery, leaving **Ovcha Kupel bus station** (❸ Ovcha Kupel Blvd, off Tsar Boris III Blvd ❶ (02) 955 5362) at 10.40 and arriving there at around 12.30. The return bus departs the monastery at 15.00, which doesn't leave you enough time for sightseeing. If possible, arrange to spend a night close to the monastery at Rilets Hotel (see page 135) or in the monastery itself (see page 134).

Many tour operators offer cheap one-day trips from Sofia to the monastery. Ask at the tourist office or at your hotel for recommendations.

SIGHTS & ATTRACTIONS

Rila Monastery

Coming from Sofia, you arrive outside the fortress-like western gate and pass through it into a serene courtyard surrounded by stylish striped arcades, tiers of monastic chambers and graceful balconies. Climb the staircase to the top balcony to take in the scenery. The monastery's kitchen, in the west wing to the left of the church that

● *Emerald lakes in the Rila Mountains*

occupies the centre of the courtyard, is well worth a visit.

The church museum is to be found in the east wing. Its claim to fame is a late 18th-century wooden cross, intricately inscribed with 140 biblical scenes and 1,500 human figures, the work of one monk who devoted 12 years of his life to the task and lost his eyesight as a consequence of spending hours squinting through a magnifying glass. ⓐ 27 km (16¾ miles) east of Rila village, off the E79, 20 km (12½ miles) south of Dupnitsa ⓣ (07054) 2208 ⓦ www.rilamonastery.pmg-blg.com ⓛ 06.00–22.00 summer; 08.00–18.00 winter; museum: 08.00–18.00. Admission charge for museum (monastery free)

Rila Monastery Church

Built in the 1830s and the largest monastery church in the country, the exterior is covered in murals and the interior walls are adorned with frescoes, all of which invite close scrutiny for their pictorial

THE HISTORY OF THE MONASTERY

The monastery owes its origins to Ivan Rilski, now known as St John of Rila, a ninth-century hermit monk who acquired a band of devotees after lengthy sojourns in the wild, and eventually founded a hermitage in the Rila Mountains. The first monastery, a short distance from the original hermitage, was founded in 1335 and became a major spiritual centre during the Middle Ages. It survived for half a millennium until it was accidentally burned down in the 19th century; rebuilding started within a year and what you see today was added to UNESCO's list of World Heritage Sites in the early 1980s.

spectacles and wealth of detail. 🕐 06.00–22.00 summer; 08.00–18.00 winter

Rila Mountains

Quite apart from the attractions of the monastery itself, hiking the rural trails through the surrounding forests is reason enough to make an excursion to this famous valley in the Rila Mountains. A number of trails start from near the monastery and the shortest, less than an hour's walk, leads to St John of Rila's cave. This route begins 2 km (1¼ miles) east of the monastery's eastern gate (the main entrance to the monastery is through the western gate) by taking the trail that heads left just after the Bachkova Cheshma restaurant. When you reach the cave, you can walk through it and come out the other side but it is unlit and very claustrophobic.

The main trails through the Rila Mountains are set out on a noticeboard in the monastery's car park, and a bracing walk can be enjoyed by taking any one of them.

TAKING A BREAK

Rila Monastery Bakery £ A monkish repast of *mekitsi* (deep-fried doughnuts), bread and sheep's milk yoghurt. 🅐 Outside the east gate of Rila Monastery 🕐 06.00–22.00 summer; 08.00–18.00 winter

Restaurant Drushlyavitsa £–££ This is easily the most attractive place for a meal when visiting Rila Monastery: a scenic location with outdoor tables taking advantage of the views and a full menu of Bulgarian dishes and fresh trout. 🅐 Outside the east gate of Rila Monastery 🕐 0888 278756 🕐 08.00–22.00

ACCOMMODATION

Rila Monastery £ Spartan accommodation in monks' cells is available at the monastery but you will have to do without hot water. Check what time the monastery gates close and plan accordingly for dinner. ❶ 0896 872010 Ⓦ www.rilamonastery.pmg-blg.com

Rilets £ A 15-minute walk from the eastern gate of Rila Monastery brings you to this featureless but functional hotel. It would do for a one-night stopover and there is a restaurant, although it would be better to eat at Restaurant Drushlyavitsa (see page 133) and get back to the hotel before dark. ❸ Rila Monastery area ❶ (07054) 2106

🔽 *You can stay overnight at Rila Monastery*

Koprivshtitsa

The small town of Koprivshtitsa played a key role in the April Uprising, an insurrection against Ottoman rule in 1876, and contains several houses of historical interest. The best museum house to see from the outside is Oslekov House; the best interior is Lyutov House. Try to avoid visiting the town on Monday and Tuesday, when many of the house museums are closed.

Make your first stop the **tourist information office** (ⓐ 20 April Square 6 ❶ (07184) 2191 ⏰ 09.00–18.00; times may vary) in the northwest corner of the main square. Two doors up is the **Kupchiynitsa**, or museums' office (⏰ 09.00–17.00), where you can purchase a combined ticket (5lv) for the town's six museum houses; this saves money if you visit more than two of them. Individual tickets (2lv) are also available.

GETTING THERE

Koprivshtitsa is 110 km (68 miles) east of Sofia, It takes about two hours to reach it by public transport, using one of the minibuses that depart daily in the morning from the Trafik-Market bus terminal next to the Central Railway Station (see page 52). The bus stop in Koprivshtitsa is in the middle of town. Follow the river northwards to reach the main 20 April Square.

SIGHTS & ATTRACTIONS

Oslekov House

This house was built in the middle of the 19th century for a rich merchant family, and the façade is painted with cityscapes of Rome,

▲ *Mother of local poet Dimcho Debelyanov waits for him to return from WWI*

Venice and Padua – places visited by the merchant. A timber staircase leads to a hall, and a set of rooms laid out with exhibits relating to the history of the house and the lifestyle of its inhabitants. The house is a couple of minutes away on foot and uphill from 20 April Square. ⓐ Hadzhi Nencho Palaveev Blvd 39 ⓣ (01784) 2555 ⓛ 09.30–17.00 Tues–Sun. Admission charge

Dimcho Debelyanov House

From Oslekov House, continue uphill and turn the corner into Dimcho Debelyanov Street to find this house on the left-hand side after 100 m (110 yds). Birthplace of the poet Dimcho Debelyanov (1887–1916), the exhibits on display relate to his tragic life but the captions are woefully inadequate. Debelyanov was killed in World War I, and his love life was marred by the early death of a woman whose father killed her to prevent her relationship with Debelyanov continuing. ⓐ Dimcho Debelyanov St 6 ⓣ (01784) 2077 ⓛ 09.30–17.00 Tues–Sun. Admission charge

Lyutov House

Cross the bridge after leaving Todor Kableshkov Street and turn left into Nikola Belovezhdov Street to find the white-painted Lyutov House on your left after 100 m (110 yds). The home of a rich and much-travelled merchant, the interior is richly decorated with murals of European locations visited by the merchant, ornately carved ceilings and Viennese furniture. ⓐ Nikola Belovezhdov St 2 ⓣ (01784) 2138 ⓛ 09.30–17.00 Wed–Mon. Admission charge

Todor Kableshkov House

From Dimcho Debelyanov House, return and turn right to reach the top of the hill and the town cemetery. Over the grave of the

🔺 *Overlooking the town*

poet stands a statue, and the small church is also worth a visit. If you turn left after leaving the churchyard on the side opposite to where you came in, you will find Todor Kableshkov House some 40 m (44 yds) down the street on your left. The interior is devoted to displays of material relating to the April Uprising, the house

being the birthplace of the hero who began the insurrection.
ⓐ Todor Kableshkov St 8 ⓣ (01784) 2054 ⓛ 09.30–17.00 Tues–Sun.
Admission charge

TAKING A BREAK

Bulgaria £ This restaurant has a lovely terrace as well as tables in
a comfortable dining area that evokes times past. It is situated on
the main street that runs by the side of the river and links the bus
stop with 20 April Square, but at its northern end and beyond the
main square. ⓐ Hadzhi Nencho Palaveev Blvd 31 ⓣ (01784) 2183
ⓛ 09.00–22.30

Chuchura £ Easy to find, close by the bus stop, this inexpensive eatery
is very convenient if you arrive in town feeling hungry and thirsty
after the journey from Sofia. Do not be put off by the unprepossessing
exterior: the food is good and relies on traditional Bulgarian favourites.
ⓐ Hadzhi Nencho Palaveev Blvd 66 ⓣ (01784) 2712 ⓦ www.mehana.eu
ⓛ 09.00–00.00

Pod Starata Krusha £ This pub-restaurant is cheap and cheerful
and offers a good range of drinks and meals throughout the day
and evening. ⓐ Hadzhi Nencho Palaveev Blvd 56 ⓣ (01784) 2163
ⓦ www.pear.hit.bg ⓛ 08.30–00.00

AFTER DARK

RESTAURANT
Dyado Liben £ This restaurant, on the eastern side of the river and
reached by a bridge from the town square, is set in a picturesque

● *Typical Renaissance house in Koprivshtitsa*

old house with an attractive cobbled courtyard and inside seating upstairs. The food is not particularly different to what is found on other restaurant menus in Koprivshtitsa, but the old building and furnishings lend an atmosphere ideally suited for an evening out.
ⓐ Hadzhi Nencho Palaveev Blvd 47 ⓣ (01784) 2109 ⓛ 09.00–23.00

ACCOMMODATION

Accommodation can be booked at the tourist information office but there should be no problem finding a place to stay. Hotels, usually small family-run affairs, are dotted around town and room rates are fairly uniform and very affordable.

Astra £ A family-run guesthouse with comfortable, traditionally decorated rooms and a pretty courtyard where you can sit with a beer or two and see the evening out. It's at the northeast corner of the village, 500 m (550 yds) from the town square across the river. ⓐ Hadzhi Nencho Palaveev Blvd 11 ⓣ (01784) 2033
ⓦ www.hotelastra.org

Bashtina Kushta £ If you want a break from the folksy style that characterises most places in town, this modern hostelry fits the bill. Uncomplicated rooms and attic ones with sloping ceilings. Walk north from the town square and it is on your left after 150 m (164 yds). ⓐ Hadzhi Nencho Palaveev Blvd 32 ⓣ (01784) 3033
ⓦ www.fhhotel.info

ⓞ *Sofia is a short flight away from the UK*

PRACTICAL
information

Directory

GETTING THERE

By air

British Airways and Bulgaria Air fly direct from London (3 hours and 20 minutes) but their fares are expensive. Wizz Air flies direct from Luton with reasonable fares as well as easyJet from Gatwick. Indirect fares via other European cities, and with other airlines, offer the best fare deals. Malév Hungarian Airlines, for example, flies to Sofia via Budapest from the UK and Ireland. Also, check out specialist agents like Balkan Holidays and compare their prices.

Balkan Holidays Ⓦ www.balkanholidays.co.uk

British Airways Ⓦ www.britishairways.com

Bulgaria Air Ⓦ www.bulgaria-air.co.uk

easyJet Ⓦ www.easyjet.com

Malév Ⓦ www.malev.hu

Regent Holidays Ⓦ www.regent-holidays.co.uk

Wizz Air Ⓦ www.wizzair.com

Travellers from North America, Australia and New Zealand should fly first to a major European air transport hub, and from there to Sofia.

Many people are aware that air travel emits CO_2, which contributes to climate change. You may be interested in the possibility of lessening the environmental impact of your flight through **Climate Care** (Ⓦ www.climatecare.org), which offsets your CO_2 by funding environmental projects around the world.

By rail

There are various rail routes but, at the moment, it is still not possible to buy a through train ticket to Sofia. The closest you can get is a booked ticket to Budapest and, once there, no problem should arise booking a ticket for the daily Budapest–Sofia train service. It will take about 24 hours to reach Budapest from London (Eurostar to Paris and on from there by sleeper via Vienna or Munich), and the last leg of the journey, Budapest–Sofia, will take that long again. Some informative sites to check out are:

The Man in Seat 61 Ⓦ www.seat61.com

Rail Europe Ⓦ www.raileurope.co.uk (UK) www.eurorailways.com (US)

Thomas Cook European Rail Timetable ⓘ (01733) 416477 (UK) Ⓦ www.thomascookpublishing.com

Trainseurope UK ⓘ 0871 700 7722 Ⓦ www.trainseurope.co.uk

By road

Arriving by car is not a feasible option: it would take forever and cost a fortune in petrol.

ENTRY FORMALITIES

In terms of visa requirements, citizens of the UK, Ireland, the US, Australia, New Zealand, Canada and other EU citizens can visit Bulgaria without a visa for 90 days. Officially, visitors from other than EU countries are required to register as a foreigner with the local police within five days of arrival, but if you are staying in a hotel or hostel this piece of bureaucracy should be done for you and you may be given a completed registration form to keep in your passport. In theory, you could be fined for not having the form when you depart, but in practice no attention is paid to this for short-stay foreigners from Western countries.

You are not allowed to export antiques or art works without a permit issued by the Ministry of Culture, and this should be arranged by the shop concerned. Import limits for EU and non-EU travellers include 1 litre of spirits or wine and 200 cigarettes.

MONEY

The Bulgarian currency is the lev, plural leva (lv), divided into 100 stotinki. The dominations for notes are 2, 5, 10, 20, 50 and 100 leva; there are coins in denominations of 1 lev and 1, 2, 5, 10, 20 and 50 stotinki. The euro is sometimes accepted (including by taxi drivers from the airport) because the lev is pegged to the European currency and there are no fluctuations. There are plans for Bulgaria eventually to adopt the euro, but this is unlikely to happen before 2012 or 13 at the very earliest.

It is not easy to obtain Bulgarian currency outside of the country, but there is no need to do so as ATMs are to be found at the airport and outside banks throughout the city. There are limits on how much can be withdrawn on any one day, and for this reason alone it makes sense to bring some cash in your home currency with you. It helps to have more than one bank debit card and/or, as a backup, some Thomas Cook or American Express traveller's cheques in sterling, US dollars or euros. Money can be exchanged at banks (between 09.00 and 16.00 Mon–Fri), and private exchange bureaux are also dotted around the city centre, although rates vary and should be checked (the ones on Vitosha Boulevard are best avoided). Credit cards are accepted in larger shops and restaurants.

In the Communist era there used to be a black market for the Bulgarian currency, and you may still find yourself approached by someone claiming to offer an exchange rate way above the official one. This will almost certainly be a scam and, through sleight of hand, you will find yourself with a wad of paper topped with one genuine banknote.

HEALTH, SAFETY & CRIME

There are no compulsory vaccinations. Tap water is chlorinated

⬥ *Police boxes are located at all major road junctions*

and safe for brushing teeth, but for drinking it is best to use the bottled water that is available everywhere in the city. Should you suffer from a mild stomach complaint or diarrhoea, pharmacies sell standard treatments and oral rehydration salts. Pharmacies may have English-speaking staff, but don't rely on this – if you require attention and prescription drugs head for a private medical clinic or hospital. See the 'Emergencies' section (page 154) for contact details.

Sofia is safer than most major European cities, but common sense dictates safety precautions with regard to personal possessions and safety. Pickpockets operate in crowded places in the city centre.

Keep a list of the numbers of your traveller's cheques with your proof of purchase (which will be needed for a claim), and the contact number to use in case the cheques are lost or stolen. Store this

⬤ A typical street kiosk

information separately from the cheques themselves; posting them to an email account is a good idea. Retain a photocopy of the main page of your passport and keep this separate from your passport. Consider storing the number of your passport, or a scanned copy of the relevant pages, in an email that can be retrieved if necessary.

OPENING HOURS

Museums and attractions are usually open 10.00–18.00, with some closing on Mondays. Government office hours are 08.30–17.00 Mon–Fri. Bank hours are 09.00–16.00, Mon–Fri. General shopping hours are 09.00–19.00, Mon–Sat, but many stay open until 20.00, the shopping malls till 22.00. Most of the shops in the city centre also open on Sunday. Markets open from around 08.30 to around 18.30. The small kiosks, which are a characteristic feature of the city, sell drinks, snacks, phone cards and a variety of other items, and tend to stay open until 21.00 or 22.00.

TOILETS

Public toilets, especially clean ones, are not common in Sofia, although you can find decent ones at Tsentralni Hali (see page 75), and in the TZUM shopping mall (see page 74). Hotels and good restaurants can always be used if necessary. At some places you might be charged for using the toilet.

CHILDREN

There are not many sights or attractions that are obviously suited to children, and time spent in old churches and museums is likely to bore them. The parks offer open space, and there is a play area in Borisova Gradina (see page 104). A trip to Mount Vitosha (see page 116) should prove engaging for energetic children and, if new to skiing, they could be introduced to the sport at Aleko. Trips on the chairlift and cable car will be fun, although with young children beware of the fact that the safety bar at the Dragalevtsi chairlift needs to be manually set by the rider. Cinema screenings are worth checking for suitable movies, and the Galaxy Bowling alley (see page 37) offers fun for all the family.

Sofia is generally a child-friendly place, and there are no problems with hotels and restaurants. For baby food and disposable nappies, use the bigger pharmacies. Finding suitable food should not be difficult and, although children's menus are rare, there will usually be suitable dishes, and familiar Western fast-food franchises can be found in the city. At the Sunday brunch at Flannagans in Radisson Blu Grand Hotel (see page 42) a children's buffet is provided and there is a supervised children's area with video screenings. Children are defined as being under 12 years of age.

COMMUNICATIONS
Internet
Internet cafés have almost disappeared from the scene in Sofia, since almost all hotels and very many cafés, restaurants and bars now offer free Wi-Fi internet access. If you want to get online during your stay, it's a good idea to bring a laptop; if not, ask at the tourist office or at your hotel for the nearest option.

Phone
The easiest and cheapest way to make phone calls is to purchase a prepaid SIM card from one of the three local operators (M-Tel, Vivacom, Globul) and insert it in your mobile phone. Network coverage is good. If you're only there for a short visit, you can also use your existing SIM card – however, check with your home

TELEPHONING BULGARIA

The international country code for Bulgaria is 359 and the city code for Sofia is 02. To call a number in Sofia, dial your international access code (00 from the UK, 011 from the US), followed by 2, followed by the seven-digit local number.

TELEPHONING ABROAD

Dial 00, which is the international access code, followed by your country code and then the area code minus the initial zero, followed by the number itself. Major country codes are: Australia: 61; Canada: 1; France: 33; Germany: 49; Ireland: 353; New Zealand: 64; South Africa: 27; UK: 44; USA: 1.

network about the cost of making and receiving calls and text messages as they can be exorbitantly high. Likewise, calls made from hotel rooms are very expensive.

Although payphones are being phased out, you may still be able to find a card-operated public phone. Mobika (blue) and Bulfon (orange) phones each use their own phone cards, which can be purchased from kiosks and used for long-distance calls. You can make cheap international calls at **Planetphone** (ⓐ Stefan Karadza St 18B, one block south of Gurko St near the post office ① (02) 980 2875 Ⓦ www.planetphone.net ⊕ 10.00–20.00 Mon–Fri, 11.00–19.00 Sat & Sun).

Post

The Central Post Office is located at Gurko Street 6 (① (02) 980 1225 ⊕ 07.00–20.30 Mon–Sat, 08.00–13.00 Sun). See the Sveta Nedelya

● *Sign for Bulgarian post*

map on page 65. Postboxes can be recognised by the distinctive brown lion/horn symbol on a yellow background.

ELECTRICITY

Electricity in Bulgaria is at 220 volts, 50Hz. Plugs have the standard European two round prongs so UK and US appliances will need an adaptor. You can buy adaptors at airports or electrical shops in the city. See Ⓦ www.kropla.com for more information.

TRAVELLERS WITH DISABILITIES

Sofia is not yet geared up for travellers with severe disabilities. Most museums and other places of interest, including churches, are not easily accessible for visitors using wheelchairs, and streets and pavements can be cracked and uneven. Disabled toilets are rare and public transport can present a challenge. However, mid- and top-range hotels usually have lifts and other facilities and should be able to offer a room which is more or less accessible. Make sure you talk to an English-speaking manager about your needs and reconfirm your wishes in an email before arrival.

TOURIST INFORMATION

There is a tourist information centre in Sofia but it's not stunning: don't expect your enquiries to be answered, nor to find a wide choice of maps and guides. ❷ Sveta Nedelya Sq 1 (next to Happy Bar & Grill) ❶ (02) 987 9778 ❸ 09.00–17.00 Mon–Fri

Some useful tourist websites are:
Ⓦ www.insidesofia.com
Ⓦ www.programata.bg
Ⓦ www.bulgariatravel.org
Ⓦ www.bgmaps.com
Ⓦ www.sofiaecho.com

BACKGROUND READING

A Ballad for Georg Henig by Victor Paskov. A highly personal novel set in 1950s Sofia by the late Victor Paskov, one of Bulgaria's most controversial contemporary authors.

A Concise History of Bulgaria by R J Crampton. The most concise and readable account of the country's amazing history.

The Balkan Cookbook by Trish Davies, Lesley Chamberlain. A guide to the cuisines of Romania, Bulgaria and the Balkan Countries.

The World is Big and Salvation Lurks Around the Corner by Ilija Trojanow. The popular Bulgarian-German author's bestselling autobiographical book was dramatised as a film in 2008.

Emergencies

The following are emergency free-call numbers:

Ambulance 🛈 150

Fire 🛈 160

Police 🛈 166

Any emergency from a mobile phone 🛈 112

MEDICAL SERVICES

The emergency hospital for Sofia is known as **Pirogov** (🅰 Totleben Blvd 21, opposite the Rodina Hotel 🛈 (02) 915 4411). Staff cannot be relied on to speak English. Private medical clinics include **Thorax** (🅰 Alexander Stamboliyski Blvd 57 🛈 (02) 912 85 🕒 24 hrs).

🔺 *Mount Vitosha first aid station*

EMERGENCY PHRASES

Help!
Помощ!
Pomosht!

Fire!
Пожар!
Pozhar!

Stop!
Спри!
Spri!

Call an ambulance/a doctor/the police/the fire brigade!
Извикайте линейка/лекар/полиция/пожарна!
Izvikayte lineyka/lekar/politsiya/pozharna!

If you need a dentist, visit **Medstom** (Knyaz Alexander Dondukov Blvd 26 (02) 981 0000 08.00–00.00) or **Juniordent** (Patriarh Evtimii Blvd 1 (02) 988 3175 07.30–19.30 Mon–Fri).

24-hour pharmacies can be found at **Ana** (Vitosha Blvd 95 (02) 953 4157), **Saldzhi** (Vitosha Blvd 35 (02) 980 5896) and **Remedium** (Graf Ignatiev St 52–54 (02) 980 6691).

EMBASSIES & CONSULATES

See www.embassyworld.com for a full list of embassies and consulates.

Australia Trakia St 37 (02) 946 1334 www.embassy.gov.au
For emergencies, contact the British embassy
Ireland Bacho Kiro St 26–30 (02) 985 3425
www.embassyofireland.bg
South Africa Bacho Kiro Street 26 (02) 939 5015
www.saembassybulgaria.com
UK Moskovska St 9 (02) 933 9222 http://ukinbulgaria.fco.gov.uk
USA Koziak St 16 (02) 937 5100 http://bulgaria.usembassy.gov

Editorial/project management: Lisa Plumridge
Copy editor: Monica Guy
Layout/DTP: Alison Rayner

The publishers would like to thank the following individuals and
organisations for supplying their copyright photographs for this book:
BigStockPhoto.com (Radoslav Stoilov, page 131; Ivo Velinov, page 7);
Axel Cleeremans, page 108; Dreamstime.com (Nikolay Dimitrov,
pages 68 & 141; Monica Farling, page 81; Borislav Ivanov, pages 5 & 154;
Mlan61, page 10; Pawel Strykowski, pages 30 & 101; Branko Veinovic,
page 111); Kalin Eftimov/123rf.com, page 143; Alan Grant, page 139;
iStockPhoto.com (Valerie Crafter, page 61; Yana Downing, page 13;
Todor Marholev, page 46); Donald Judge, page 85; Klearchos Kapoutsis,
pages 115 & 126; Polia Mihaylova, pages 15, 21 & 86; Zeynep Mufti,

Send your thoughts to
books@thomascook.com

- **Found a great bar, club, shop or must-see sight that we don't feature?**
- **Like to tip us off about any information that needs a little updating?**
- **Want to tell us what you love about this handy little guidebook and
  more importantly how we can make it even handier?**

Then here's your chance to tell all! Send us ideas, discoveries and
recommendations today and then look out for your valuable input
in the next edition of this title.

Email the above address (stating the title) or write to:
pocket guides Series Editor, Thomas Cook Publishing, PO Box 227,
Coningsby Road, Peterborough PE3 8SB, UK.

WHAT'S IN YOUR GUIDEBOOK?

Independent authors Impartial up-to-date information from our travel experts who meticulously source local knowledge.

Experience Thomas Cook's 165 years in the travel industry and guidebook publishing enriches every word with expertise you can trust.

Travel know-how Thomas Cook has thousands of staff working around the globe, all living and breathing travel.

Editors Travel-publishing professionals, pulling everything together to craft a perfect blend of words, pictures, maps and design.

You, the traveller We deliver a practical, no-nonsense approach to information, geared to how you really use it.

page 51; Margarit Ralev/SXC.hu, page 152; Sheraton Sofia Hotel Balkan, pages 40–1 & 67; Meeli Tamm, pages 33, 35, 62, 63 & 147; Phil Wigglesworth, pages 17, 94, 96–7, 99, 107 & 137; Jason Wojcechowskyj, page 76; Sean Sheehan, all others.

Useful phrases

English	Bulgarian	Approx pronunciation
BASICS		
Yes	Да	*Dah*
No	Не	*Neh*
Please	Моля	*Molya*
Thank you	Благодаря	*Blagodarya*
Hello	Здравейте	*Zdraveiteh*
Goodbye	Довиждане	*Dovizhdaneh*
Excuse me	Извинете	*Izvinete*
Sorry	Съжалявам	*Sazhalyavam*
That's okay	Няма проблеми	*Nyama problemi*
I don't speak Bulgarian	Не говоря български	*Ne govoryah bulgarski*
Do you speak English?	Говорите ли английски	*Govorite li angliyski?*
Good morning	Добро утро	*Dobro utro*
Good afternoon	Добър ден	*Dobar den*
Good evening	Добър вечер	*Dobar vecher*
Goodnight	Лека нощ	*Lekah nosht*
My name is ...	Казвам се ...	*Kazvam se ...*
NUMBERS		
One	Едно	*Edno*
Two	Две	*Dveh*
Three	Три	*Trih*
Four	Четири	*Chetiri*
Five	Пет	*Pet*
Six	Шест	*Shess*
Seven	Седем	*Sedem*
Eight	Осем	*Osem*
Nine	Девет	*Devet*
Ten	Десет	*Desset*
Eleven	Единайсет	*Edinaiset*
Twelve	Дванайсет	*Dvanaiset*
Twenty	Двайсет	*Dvaiset*
Fifty	Петдесет	*Petdesset*
One hundred	Сто	*Stoh*
SIGNS & NOTICES		
Airport	Летище/Аерогара	*Letishteh/Aerogara*
Railway station	Ж. П. Гара	*Zh. P. Gara*
Platform	Перон	*Peron*
Smoking/ No smoking	За пушачи/ Пушенето забранено	*Za pushachi/ Pusheneto zabraneno*
Toilets	Тоалетната	*Toaletnata*
Ladies/Gentlemen	Жени/Мъже	*Zheni/Muzheh*
Tram/bus/metro	Трамвай/автобус/метро	*Tramvay/avtobus/metro*